FRANCE

An Illustrated Miscellany

FRANCE

An Illustrated Miscellany

Denis Tillinac

Series edited by
Jean-Claude Simoën and Ghislaine Bavoillot

Plon | Flammarion

Contents

7   *Preface*: In Praise of France

21   Auriac

25   Napoleon Bonaparte

28   Bordeaux

32   Millet's *Angelus*

35   Champagne

41   De Gaulle's Resting Place

42   Proust's Combray

46   The Rooster

50   Country Roads

54   Deux Chevaux

57   Dordogne

65   French Writers

73   Fabulous La Fontaine

76   The Frenchwoman

82   Train Stations

87   A French Feast

94   Henry IV

99   The Impressionists

109   Joan of Arc

113   Brasserie Lipp

114   The Loire

128   A Family Home

132   "La Marseillaise"

134   The Sea

146   Tintin's Marlinspike Hall

150   Notre-Dame Cathedral

155   Baguette

157   Paris, Queen of the World

170   Basque Country

174   Édith Piaf

177   Provence

190   Mealtimes

195   The Riviera

205   Saint-Denis Cathedral

206   Sainte-Chapelle

208   A Walk along the Seine

217   Bayeux Tapestry

219   The TGV

222   Tour de France

228   Versailles

236   Wine

242   Volcanoes

249   The *Zinc*

Page 2   July 14 at Le Havre. Raoul Dufy painted this street awash with banners in 1906.

Facing page   Blue, white, red: in this famous portrait by Jean Fouquet, painter to Charles VII, representing the king's favorite as the Virgin, the seraphim are blue, Agnès Sorel's breasts white, and the angels red.

In Praise of France

I adore France body and soul, like a star-struck wooer, a blissful lover. She is my glorious muse. I fantasize about her, I idealize her, but her dales and vales still fill me with the most earthly desires. As I crisscross this land, as I embrace it, it never fails to astonish me: it's physical. I love to locate the gold and the blood of her history deep in the flesh of her geology. The patriotism that results from this is of a rustic vein; a kind of blind faith.

Some forge their patriotism in the unyielding metal of a concept; mine is modeled from the clay of my dreams. I am French, plain and simple. And I derive from the fact as much pride as pleasure. I have for this ancient nation the love of a perfect knight for a high-born lady, of a buccaneer for a servant girl at the inn, of a scholar for his dusty tomes, of a farmer for his plot of land, of an investor for his dividends, of the faithful for a relic of their patron saint.

My love for France is easygoing. Like others' for a wine that makes them tipsy. France is lodged within my heart; she sticks to my boots. I confess being French in both mind and soul; it's all been quite involuntary and effortless. But not obsessive. And always a delight. Things might have been different and I am very conscious of what I would have lost had this been the case. On occasion I have grumbled about being let loose on this Earth bang in the middle of the twentieth century; rightly or wrongly, I think I would be better suited to some other era. But I have never regretted being born French, even if it periodically dawns on me that my compatriots hardly deserve the privilege. I am a common-or-garden Frenchman; native-born and glad of this piece of good luck.

As far as you go back up my family tree, on my mother's and my father's side, my genetic pool is bordered by the fringes of the Massif

Facing page   The bell tower at the abbey of Conques, now a UNESCO World Heritage site.
Pages 8–9   "Come-hither Paris languishes voluptuously on the banks of the Seine." D. T.
Pages 10–11   "Even without Courbet the place would still be magical." D. T.
Gustave Courbet stayed at Étretat and painted this cliff in 1869.

Central. A great-grandfather upped sticks from Burgundy and planted them in the province of the Bourbonnais. For the rest, it was Auvergne and the borders of the Limousin. Gergovie is never far off. I particularly adore two villages on the Gallic map, but all around and every which way I find France: Oceanic, Latin, Flemish, Northern around the edges, Germanic in the marches, and then Paris, where everything converges. In point of fact, I was born and bred in the capital, like so many Frenchmen whose ancestors "went up" to Paris with a pair of clogs, a battered suitcase, and their ambitions and illusions. Our provinces are full of character and memories, but they all gravitate around the metropolis like moths around a lamp.

All the material for my authorial excursions has come free with these roots. My down-to-earth, plebian soul has long regaled in a measure of sovereignty over a few acres between two bell towers. And I know well where "the play is ended." My ancestors lie in a heap in the graveyard, together with other families. It provides one with perspective and, in the end, a measure of nonchalance. Since I am to join them soon, it's almost like I was already there.

To be able to withdraw emotionally to the flanks of a vast primary mountain range is an incalculable advantage. Though I've never whipped it into an ideology. "The soil and its dead." That's not for me. For my kind of patriotism, it all seems half-baked. My love for France is in no way regionally based, and it is too solidly embedded to get contorted into identity politics. Why make such a fuss about an "identity," anyhow. It flows as from a spring, oozes like sap. It's a humus; not a bunker. Someone can be French and hail from elsewhere. In fact, we are always a bit from elsewhere and no Frenchman can be too sure of which ancestor makes his blood run clear.

The first article of my patriotic credo is as simple as ABC: France is by far the best thing history and geography have come up with on all five continents. The most beautiful, the most noble, the most lip-smacking. Once this axiom is posited, no need to try and ram it home. Instead of confining me, my roots have sprouted into a search for universality; hence my unquenchable thirst for the far-away and the marginal, for the deep south, for nomadic peoples, for traveling circuses, for the racial mix. While I remain French through and through, my desire for otherness is unbounded. Nothing could be dumber than the denigration of "horizontal" France by opposing it to the mirage of an abstract, lifeless "verticality." Typical of the chattering classes, it is the spawn of their

airy conceptualizing. In claiming liberation from the bonds essential to every population, in fact they betray a cliquey disdain for the people. In reality, France results from both rootedness *and* unrootedness. The sedentary nature of its inhabitants, tributary of thousands of years of rural life in the West, has always been counterbalanced by a mysterious drive to wander far and wide from their glebe.

From the very dawn of its destiny, this population of plowmen, saber-rattlers, and tub-thumpers has distilled its desires into ideals. Not always advisedly. When the Angelus sounds, France and her belfries gaze up at heaven, but the stars that shine there are not just ours—they come from a land without borders, one that any mortal man can inhabit. Though, for it to bear fruit, any union between the senses and the soil needs to keep its bell towers.

Racism, nationalism, regionalism, atavism: all of these scaremongering *-isms* are more foreign to me than any foreigner. I put internationalism in the same box. There are no *-isms* in this book, and no ideology either. The France I love is not based on theory: it is a magic lantern that satisfies my cravings with stunningly sumptuous scenery, with highly colored characters, with elaborate pipedreams, with a weft and weave of mighty deeds and tall stories, all clouded with regret, for one would like France to be unsullied, but her memory is besmirched by blood.

The pleasure I derive from the good fortune of being born French is limitless. I live in France, I explore her tirelessly. I read her writers, her historians, her local antiquarians, her newspapers, her shop signs. I love her every day, as with a lover soft to the touch, easy on the eye, gentle to one's inner self—like a Circe capable of every metamorphosis. I use her language with relish, a language that has allowed me, at least, to become one of the figures to which I aspired: a French author.

Wherever I go a-courting France, she enchants me. I will never tire of possessing her, body and soul. Cajoling Paris with its necklace of provinces; her towns and boroughs, her nooks and crannies, her spells. France is a fountain of youth, a multifaceted mirror. Traveling from place to place, I never take the same road twice; I'm afraid of dying without seeing some manor house nestling behind antediluvian oaks, or a snatch of landscape standing out against the horizon. I never enter a church without caressing its stonework with the tips of my fingers, and never leave a handsome village without promising to return.

When the children were still at school, we would, at the end of summer, embark on the exploration of some French region. They'll go to the US in good time, I told myself. I wanted them to know the highlights of our heritage, at least by sight. I was driven by a sense of duty—not something I am generally overburdened with. The châteaux of the Loire, the ossuary at Douaumont, the bridge over the Gard, Mont Saint-Michel, the arena at Nîmes, Locronan, Conques, Riquewihr, the needle of Étretat, Domrémy, the gorges of the Tarn, the *hospices* of Beaune, Cordes, and Gordes, as well as Les Baux-de-Provence and Beaumont-en-Auge, the Baie des Anges, Mont Sainte-Odile and Alphonse Daudet's windmill at Fontvieille, cathedrals, *bastides*, distant shores: I inflicted the lot on them. On reaching the *nth* monument, we had to curtail our odyssey: they couldn't have cared less then about Diane de Poitiers, Vauban's fortifications, or the saints on the tympanum at Chartres. Exacting their revenge, in the car they would bawl 1980s teen pop, and, to restore a semblance of peace, I had to promise them swimming pools and TV galore. I regret none of this: neither do they now. Apart from the pleasure of us all being together, these journeys left them with a hazy sense that their homeland harbors fabulous treasures. Almost as fabulous as their own village. Sooner or later, they will return to gaze again on what they absorbed, and then they will be even prouder of being French. None of this will prevent them from traveling to all four corners of the earth: the world is vast and there is ample material for poetry under every sun. I've kicked about a bit myself, often with delight and never without learning something. But nothing has overwhelmed me as much as the architectural and scenic jewels of France: in comparison with Chambord, the beauty of the Taj Mahal seemed almost insignificant. And the same goes for all the rest.

To accompany my love for France, lush strings would be ridiculous and a Requiem Mass unseemly: the couple she and I form have lived like newlyweds, and, whatever people may say here and there, her "identity" is in fine fettle. That Western civilization, from which the nation of France springs, may be in a calamitous state is something else entirely. Even supposing that civilization collapses—alas, an all too plausible hypothesis—the soul of France will remain intact. She cannot die. The beat of her heart within me remains full of the joys of spring. Perhaps it is France that will allow future generations of the world to rebuild on the ruins. Or perhaps not. In the meantime, for me France is the most

gorgeous country in the world, the most refined, the wittiest, the pleasantest to live in. Despite their faults the French possess inexhaustible reserves of vigor, shrewdness, and generosity. And I write this cognizant of the gloom and doom that periodically engulf my compatriots. They have a penchant for self-criticism and another for nihilism. They are even masochistic enough to convince themselves that the grass is greener on the other side and, according to fashion, have been infected with a mania for the USSR or for England. They search for "life answers" in Kathmandu, Havana, or the Silicon Valley. They get over it as fast as they caught it: it's just a symptom of a kind of puerile changeability that did not escape the eagle eye of Julius Caesar. And in any case, all this only concerns the "elites": the bulk of the troops are happy to live in France, be it on a square of asphalt. French people are not ones to emigrate and if they do, it's never for long: it takes the carrot of a fat bonus to make them deign to leave home.

From time immemorial the bell in my village has rung the hours, monotonous, languorous. As I listen to it intone, in the timeless silence, the entire history of France parades before me: a long line of knights and wights, of beggars and churchmen whose epic tale not only moves me, it also presents me with an obligation, for to be born French is no insignificant matter. Fifteen centuries or more have bestowed on us a role in the world. But which one? No one knows, but the feeling sneaks up on us that such an extraordinary privilege cannot come without responsibilities. Since derring-do is out of the question, the age of chivalry being apparently over and done with, it is our task as Frenchmen to remain conscious of our felicity and proclaim our good fortune from the rooftops. This book would like nothing better than to be a song of joy and a gift of thanks. I want to write it as I breathe—like a man in love.

Denis Tillinac

Pages 14–15 The charm of Corrèze lies in the beauty of its opulent scenery.
Facing page "Do not forget to see the most famous châteaux of the Loire Valley once again." D. T.
The Château de Chambord.
Page 18 A house in Corrèze on the way to Santiago de Compostela.

The sun is never
as beautiful
as the day
when you set out
on the road.

Jean Giono, *Les Grands Chemins*

Auriac

A sun from the age of Genesis emerges from behind the bluish peaks of the chain of the Puys mountains. Crisp hoarfrost sparkles in the dawn. Like cream, the fog rises from the gorge and between the bare branches of the cherry tree one glimpses the bell tower that sounds the hours. Always the same hours since my childhood, so that the procession of time, with its gentle melancholy, suggests eternity over loss. This is my village, Auriac. It takes patience to locate on a roadmap this little, gray granite town roofed in *lauze* stone, gathered around a squat church with a keep that makes it look like a fort. This is no longer the Limousin, almost no longer the Corrèze, and not quite the Auvergne. Out in the sticks, yet at the center of the world. Perched on a plateau called the Xaintrie, it does not seem unhappy with its lot. All around, sloping meadows where the schist breaks through the daisies. Fern and broom, paths lined with hazel and mulberry trees, and brambles on the edge of dark woods watered by brooks that run down to the Dordogne river.

When the clouds billow, Wagnerian storms blast the trees, and, on occasion, the cows. Red or mahogany cows, bearing majestic horns and with a long-haired coat that makes them resemble prehistoric animals. These are Salers, renowned for their endurance, their skittish nature. When I was a child, the herds that tramped across the square before the church on their way to milking comprised solely this breed. Recently, they've been thrown together with Charolais. Ahead of the curve, my father, hooking up with a woman from the Bourbonnais, was to produce one particular mongrel among others: me. It is a writer's destiny to straddle borders.

Auriac is my haven, my den, the inner sanctum of my authorial quest. Here, I have dreamed and prayed, hoped and despaired. Here, in the soft glow of the family home, were laid the foundations of my feeling for the countryside—with the occasional assistance of an indigenous girlfriend, or one who, like me, spent the summer with a grandmother clad in black. This is my village, the inaugural theater of my phantasmagorias, the confidant of my narcissistic stirrings. The most beautiful village in the world.

Left
"My village of Auriac. It is no longer the Limousin, almost no longer the Corrèze, and not quite the Auvergne." D. T.

You write to me that it is "impossible"— that word is not French.

Napoleon Bonaparte

Napoleon Bonaparte

I would surely have hated his cynicism, his social climbing, his nepotism, his racism, his cloying sentimentality. Put end to end, the features of his personality produce a knave whom one would not want as a friend. Not even as a fellow infantryman. Like everyone else I would have been beguiled by the Italian campaign; and, doubtless, by the insane Egyptian adventure.

Perhaps I would have approved of the coup of 18 Brumaire that brought him to power: the government needed shaking up. He was a true leader and already a hero. The self-proclamation was an inevitable consequence. His coronation at Notre-Dame Cathedral would have made me giggle. So kitsch that even his (freshly minted) field marshals had to stifle a laugh. They disapproved of a masquerade that paradoxically rendered Bonapartism less stable and conducted themselves like filibusters.

Bonaparte's work as a legislator leaves one breathless: he foresaw everything, drafted everything, implemented everything. I would have admired him at this Herculean task. But the frenzy for war. Europe razed to the ground: Austerlitz, Wagram, Essling, Eylau, Spain, Russia, and the campaign in France.

Perhaps I would have joined up so as not to be left behind and become one victim among so many of his stubborn refusal to face facts. All these corpses to end up with the Treaty of Vienna and the restoration of the monarchy. Still, he had gazed on the Pyramids, slept at Schönbrunn Palace and the Kremlin: the stuff of dreams. He shook them all up: kings, princes, peoples, chiefs of staff, thinkers (Hegel). Perhaps his tyranny would have driven me into exile in the footsteps of Chateaubriand. But I might have joined him on that fabulous three-week "eagle flight from belfry to belfry" that led him from Golfe-Juan to the Élysée Palace.

Napoleon I is a great dark sun rising over our nation's melancholy. What we owe him is unimaginable, but he made us pay for it dearly, in woe and angst. In a way, the entire history of our national consciousness begins with Waterloo, on that ghastly plain.

Page 22
"Napoleon I is a great dark sun rising over our nation's melancholy." D. T.
Napoleon as the *Little Corporal*. A statue from 1833 at the Musée de l'Armée.

Facing page
"I would have been beguiled by the Italian campaign.... He was a true leader and already a hero." D. T.
Bonaparte on the Bridge of Arcole by Antoine-Jean Gros, at the Hermitage.

I could recognize Corsica from afar
with my eyes closed from her scent.

Napoleon Bonaparte

A village in Balagne, one of Corsica's most beautiful areas,
not far from where Napoleon embarked for the continent in 1793.

Bordeaux

At first blush, as one enters Bordeaux by Napoleon's Pont de Pierre, the city bordering the quayside of the River Garonne appears clad in the regular features of a facade designed by the *intendant* Tourny at the end of the eighteenth century. This is "classical" Bordeaux, with the place de la Bourse, the quarter around the Grand Théâtre, the vast place des Quinconces, and the edifices encircling the public garden. But if you sneak along the wharf in the direction of the station and slip in through a medieval gate, the Porte de la Monnaie, you'll discover, gathered around a Gothic spire and a bell tower, a more Bohemian area where Arabs who settled here long ago rub shoulders with students and pensioners.

Little by little—the tendency is inescapable—it'll all become gentrified. This has not quite come to pass yet: the district of Saint-Michel still possesses bastions of authenticity. In this city and its hinterland, surely due to the religion of wine, gastronomy forms an integral part of an aesthetic epicureanism that embraces rugby, lampreys, bullfighting, *pibale* eels, the poetry of La Ville de Mirmont, and Arcachon oysters (served with *crépinette* parcels and a Graves de Pessac-Léognan). One really has to read to be able to understand this marriage between the flesh and the spirit, celebrated by Montaigne and François Mauriac. One really has to hear chef Jean-Pierre Xiradakis evoke images from literature or art to describe the scent of a herb or a cèpe mushroom. It takes a dinner between pals at my favorite restaurant, La Tupina, to realize that Bordeaux, beneath its haughty air, splendid but stiff with pride and distorted by anglomania, conceals an almost heady sensuality. The frontages in its chicer areas and the shop-houses in its less affluent quarters seem to keep this desire in check, but, paradoxically, the gracefully blond church of Saint-Pierre lets fall a confession: Bordeaux is a foodie city.

Right
"Bordeaux's new lighting metamorphoses the place de la Bourse into a kind of fairylike and crepuscular apotheosis." D. T.

I have no clear idea of the whole world. But I sing for my own valley, and desire that every Rooster may do the same for his.

Edmond Rostand, *Chantecler*

Millet's *Angelus*

It is scarcely visible in the picture, but everything converges toward it: the belfry of Chailly-en-Bière, the church that sounds the Angelus of Millet. All said and done, it heralded the death-knell of rural, Catholic France. Echoing an eternal hope, it simultaneously announced the end of a destiny. For it should be said that the austere, biblical, but not very clerical Jean-François Millet, who had known agricultural toil in his native Cotentin, had no time for rose-tinted cowpats: his reapers, harvesters, gleaners, butter-churners, and dairymaids submit to a dismal fate. I love this painting: the medieval fervor of the woman, the peasant gently bowing his head, his as it were supplicant manner of clasping his hands, the wheelbarrow to one side, the hayfork to the other, the orangey yellow of the twilight. It is the spit and image of a France of bell towers, thatched cottages, and stone crucifixes planted at the crossroads. The pious and hard-working France of the mother of poet Charles Péguy that I idealized during my Parisian exile, without ever thinking it could vanish so quickly. I just had the time to catch a fleeting glimpse of it in my own village, where it was on the way out as everywhere else in France. Its demise is far from inconsequential: the French are, more profoundly than most, a population of farmers, as the significance of agriculture in the national economy today testifies.

The writing was on the wall for rural life already under Louis-Philippe and Napoleon III. Millet and Théodore Rousseau strove to capture it in landscapes that are humble, but not cowed. Soon after, with the impressionists and their followers, came the age of the countryside as backdrop. I adore this plain magnified in the twilight by Rousseau, who lodged the members of the Barbizon School and inspired them to take over where the School of Fontainebleau had left off. Their search for nature moves me: tree trunks by Camille Corot, Antoine-Louis Barye's poplars in the gorges of Apremont, then Paul Cézanne's landscapes. Chailly has conserved some of its soul and one can almost smell it at the sign of the Cheval-Blanc inn, where the walls are lined with paintings. I adore the Chailly bell tower: it sounds the same antediluvian hours as the one in my village and overlooks a cemetery in which, not far from the graves of Millet and Rousseau, reposes an admirable friend of mine. In posthumous friendship, their tombs stand side by side. Rousseau's is just a jumble of rocks, while Millet's is no great shakes either.

Champagne

Her eyes cloud over, her cheeks turn pink, her lips let slip a final "yes." At last, she succumbs! *Champagne!* Zinedine Zidane dribbles past the last defender and steadies himself to shoot; the keeper is caught wrong-footed and the winning goal for Les Bleus bulges the net. *Champagne!* If, with my buddies for the regiment, from college, or from the rugby club, I plan a foray to some good old-fashioned watering hole, it's champagne that spumes nostalgically over our salad days!

Champagne is de rigueur for family get-togethers, and if a friend's had a run of luck we dig out a bottle. Still wines have their virtues, aperitifs their role, and virile dinners call for something stronger by way of epilogue. But champagne is for life on the up, on the razzle, a devil-may-care life! When the cork leaps out at last, our heart starts beating wildly. When it bubbles up and sparkles in a glass or crystal flute, every venue turns into a pleasure dome and dull reality is soon left far behind. A strumpet morphs into a duchess, a pen-pusher into James Dean, the technocrat becomes an adventurer, a journo form the local rag into a mix of Hemingway and Orwell, while the most obscure alderman pictures himself in the Élysée Palace in the President's armchair.

Thanks to the magic of champagne, any metamorphosis is plausible. It racks up your dreams, it distills in the soul an opulence at once luxurious, voluptuous, silky, overwhelming, and heady. Admittedly, the illustrious mythology behind this wine predisposes it to appear in *fêtes galantes* against a backdrop painted by Jean-Antoine Watteau or Jean-Honoré Fragonard. But its texture, the piquant yet subtle way it titillates the tongue, its toasty, appley flavors already ensure it a place in a world where elegance is second nature. This is why it should be imbibed like an alchemical elixir, not knocked back any old how.

It can be drunk anywhere—but not at any time. The circumstances, be they unlikely, have to be just right. Paradoxically enough one can justifiably open a bottle of champagne in a stairwell, on a building site, or in a bus shelter: the point is that the pretext has to be special and the party has to take off. Brothers in arms might oil their fraternity with beer and some enthusiasms can be pushed over the edge by red wine. Champagne, though, is for

Page 30
A giant French rooster, a work by the German artist Katharina Fritsch, erected in 2013 on Trafalgar Square in London, beside the statue of Napoleon's sworn enemy, Admiral Nelson.

Pages 32–33
The Angelus by Jean-François Millet that now hangs in the Musée d'Orsay.

Facing page
Champagne! "When it bubbles up and sparkles in a glass or crystal flute, every venue turns into a pleasure dome and dull reality is soon left far behind." D. T.

elective affinities, for tête-a-tête suppers, for more intimate commemorations. The state has ordained it for winding up its banquets, and it is an essential ingredient in any cocktail worth the time of day. Its inalienable vocation, however, is not to compound a state of drunkenness, nor even to kick proceedings off. It is to instill, into the most far-flung neurons, an intoxication of our sensitivity that brings us closer to what we might have done, to what we ought to have tried, to what we should have become. And, always, drawing us upwards. In me, at least, an ordinary hangover inspires the nightmares of a grunt. The abuse of champagne, on the other, bestows on me a more elevated soul: I see myself inhabited by some exemplary destiny, accompanied by the most inspiring of muses.

We remain forever in the thrall of the pipe dreams of our youth. While still a penniless student, I already wanted to become a writer. This beguiling vision was associated with, among other advantages, the following scene: I am perched on a stool at the bar in the Ritz with a flute of champagne in my hand. Just the one to begin with, on my lonesome, the following glass being offered to me in unison by a posse of ready wits and a bevy of gorgeous nymphs. As time passed my youth evaporated. I have since spilled ink and drunk champagne, plain and pink, by the bucket load, in the Ritz and elsewhere. Has my pen gained in fluidity by being dipped into this potion? I have no clue. Still, it is my conviction that it is an essential component of our ennoblement. In this respect, it is fitting that champagne should bolster our patriotism: champagne *is* France. Anyone can point to its vineyards on a map—not far from Rheims, where the history of our country practically began. Each time I catch sight of its vines from Épernay, I am caught up in a burst of chauvinistic pride. Throughout the world, at the moment the bubbles begin to sparkle, the genius of France penetrates into the drinkers' brains and the most calamitous boor is transformed into an irresistible "French lover." It is enough for him to order another glass and he is instantly possessed by the ghosts of princes.

Facing page
"The magic of champagne! It distills in the soul an opulence at once luxurious, voluptuous, silky, overwhelming, and heady." D. T. Photograph by Frank Horvat for Pommery.

Every man has two countries:
his own and France.

Thomas Jefferson

The French tricolor lights up the streets of Paris on June 30, 1878.
A canvas by Claude Monet in the collection of the Musée des Beaux-Arts, Rouen.

De Gaulle's Resting Place

Clinging to an arid peak around a nondescript bell tower and immersed in a gloomy forest, Colombey itself is hardly a tourist magnet. A very bare, very white tomb in the cemetery next to the church. Charles de Gaulle, 1890–1970.

Girded by high walls and surrounded by a park, de Gaulle's residence, La Boisserie, is a genteel pile in a leaden, late nineteenth-century style. Seated at his desk, pen in hand, the general, letting his eye wander over the seemingly boundless woods, ruminates in fathomless melancholy. This is the East of our origins and our misfortune. Clairvaux is not far off, he must be thinking of Saint Bernard. But what remains today of the zest and inspiration of the Cistercians? Joinville is not far away either, so perhaps he's reflecting on Saint Louis. What survives of the Crusaders' dreams? Domrémy and Vaucouleurs lie on the same trajectory. What remains of Joan of Arc's redemptive innocence in that sorry age when French national prestige derived primarily from the anatomy of Brigitte Bardot in *And God Created Woman*? (Not nothing, but not enough.) Unless of course he is meditating on the senseless carnage of Verdun, when he was just another officer. His wife knits by his side. We are in the mid-1950s. The general is an old man writing his memoirs. He won the war, saved our honor, and avoided civil strife. He has left the government and will most likely never be called back. France has got bogged down in its colonies—Indochina, Algeria—while pettifogging parliamentarians indulge in mudslinging. This "France" is unworthy of France. Not that it has been often. To his way of thinking the nation resembles a vestal virgin forever soiled by shirkers, fixers, and trimmers.

For me, de Gaulle remains a romantic hero, the invincible watchtower of my patriotism. No French book published since the liberation has marked me as much as his war memoirs, the ternary rhythm of its phrases reminding me of the grandiloquent sentences of Chateaubriand. The prologue sums it up: France is a princess in a child's fairytale, whose distinguishing characteristic is grandeur. Not power: grandeur. One could say that this requirement exceeds the moral borders of French patriotism. If not, why do so many Germans and Americans come to Colombey, as contemplative in front of his tomb as if visiting a shrine?

Proust's Combray

Combray is not far from Chartres, but it corresponds to a less ecclesiastical stratum of French sensibility—that of its bourgeoisie at its zenith. Perhaps it needed a Jewish writer to mount together all its jewels into a single cameo of such a heady perfume.

Proust's *Search* makes the head spin, bewitching us with its endless sentences that roll along in diamond tears like wavelets on sand. Combray is what remains when Odette is forgotten, with Gilberte, Saint-Loup, Charlus, Bergotte, Bloch, and the others. Administratively, the town is called Illiers. The officials added the Combray: it was the least they could do. I like to arrive via Dargeau and the Ozanne Valley, through an area of the Beauce less monochrome and flat than that celebrated by Charles Péguy. The station is as it was, with a little waiting room roofed over with brick on the platform and a plane-tree-lined avenue leading to the town. Here is the sloping square, the church with its staircases, a Gothic rose window above its portal, its sturdy though elegant tower, and decorated wooden paneling with the pulpit built into it. To the rear, stained glass from the time of Marcel. Ornamented ceiling and beams. It is the church in which the Duchesse de Guermantes appeared to the bedazzled child. Here is Aunt Léonie's house, the enclosed garden, the grille where Swann rang to announce his visit.

I have never managed to identify the two *"Côtés"*—Guermantes and Méséglise—in situ, whereas, in my mind's eye, I distinguish them perfectly, each one corresponding to a precise sequence of emotions. To find the château at Tansonville, on the other hand, is child's play.

Here time flips inside-out like a glove. I forget the allotments and the highway access road that encircles Illiers. I am that sickly and insomniac child with nerves stretched taut like the strings of a lyre, who, become a writer, recomposes a universe from his nostalgic gleanings. The France Proust resuscitates, invents, is a multifaceted one: there is of course his childhood, perceived from a middle-class perspective as much in the thrall of "castes" as any African society. But then there is that *"doulce France,"* which percolates up from the most distant past, emerging from the undergrowth of consciousness just like the duchess gliding through the church to take her pew. Mirrors reflecting mirrors, the one fits

Pages 40–41
"Seated at his desk, pen in hand, the general, letting his eye wander over the seemingly boundless woods, ruminates in fathomless melancholy.... For me, de Gaulle remains a romantic hero, the invincible watchtower of my patriotism." D. T. "France cannot be France without grandeur," claimed Charles de Gaulle in his *War Memoirs* written on this very desk.

Facing page
Portrait of Marcel Proust by Jacques-Émile Blanche. "Proust's *Search* makes the head spin; it bewitches us with its endless sentences that roll along in diamond tears like wavelets on sand." D. T.

45

Proust's Combray

Facing page
"Here is Aunt Léonie's house, the enclosed garden." D. T.
The world of Marcel the child starts with the house belonging to his uncle and aunt, the Amiots, converted into a Proust museum in 1972.

into the other. The French middle-class was wrestling power from the nobility, but, throughout the nineteenth century, its aesthetic outlook took its cue from the aristocratic haunts of the Faubourg Saint-Germain. Rocked by World War I, it never had the time to gain a moral foothold of its own. Hence its precarious soul, its evanescence, and its snobbery. Proust amplifies the ambiguities of this "soul," cultivating it in a hothouse out in the sticks of the Beauce where the narrator's parents sort of had their roots. The characters he presents tend to the nondescript: his parents, grandmother, and aunt, the maidservant, Françoise. Swann, an enigmatic figure— an aesthete socially compromised by marrying below expectations—introduces an air of mystery that is only dissipated by the apparition of the duchess. Already the word is heard as if from afar. Guermantes: a melodious sound that conjures up a France of fine ladies encased in perhaps haunted castles; France before the instigation of the *tempus per annum* of Catholic liturgy, an age of endlessly replayed time-worn ritual.

Proust purveys the fantastical emanations of this poetic aristocratism (the only type bearable); it is the quintessence of the haute bourgeois soul, its apotheosis and its swansong, its ultimate offshoot before the dictatorship of the universal petit bourgeois.

Breathing in the scent of the hawthorns around Tansonville, I feel what poets long ago hinted at and what Proust went on to dissect. Waving his intellectual nerve-endings like magic lanterns, he braided the tares of snobbery into an elaborate arabesque. In every Frenchman there exists a château in some parkland in which a duchess languishes—and it doesn't matter whether her title dates back to Saint Louis or to Napoleon III, or even that she owed it to services rendered to a society madam. We are inclined to devote to her a most hopeless love. In Alain Fournier's *Lost Domain*, the "Grand Meaulnes" strove to make this fiction come true. There is in each of us a "Guermantes Way" and a "Méséglise Way" between which our desires oscillate like a malfunctioning pendulum.

I am always a little disappointed on returning from Combray: mine is more beautiful than the real one. I reread the first volume of the *Search*, *Swann's Way*, and am astonished to be so encumbered, weighed down by inexpressible regret. Not inexpressible, perhaps hidden or fallow. Memories surface from childhood revolving around a country house, in a flowering of subtle, cloying emotions that sear into me near the heart. Just an hour from Paris down the highway, Combray stands at the other end of the world.

The Rooster

In the village his song rouses me from my slumbers and conjures up the sunshine, even in the grayest dawn. It is a playful cry, blustering, mildly belligerent—a bugle call, a plea for *joie de vivre*. Self-assertion combined with naive showing-off and boyish chest-thumping.

I like the *coq gaulois*'s cock-a-doodle-doo and his plumage. I admire this pretension with which the English already identified us in the Middle Ages in an attempt to wound our pride. Crest to the wind, with threatening beak and erect on our spurs, we turned the tables on them and embraced the rooster as our national fetish!

One sees him cast in bronze on our war memorials, in red against a blue ground decorating the badge on the shirts worn by our international sports' teams, and, when "La Marseillaise" resounds, one can almost hear his raucous cry to arms, while we hens beat our wings in appreciation in the stands.

I like to see him reigning every day over his cackling womenfolk, splendidly feathered, monarch of the farmyard. There lurks in his glad eye the twinkle of the local lothario, as if he is quite sure every hen is just for him. The two Napoleons were wrong to opt for the imperial eagle: an insult to our rusticity. A Frenchman soars into the air as rarely as he mounts his high horse, preferring to remain down-to-earth whenever he has to show his teeth. But he might strut on occasion. Or fight to the death when called for. Or unaccountably burst out into song in sheer joy at living beneath a French sky.

Facing page
The Gallic rooster: "I admire this pretension with which the English already identified us in the Middle Ages." D. T. Picasso painted this *Tricolor Cockerel with the Cross of Lorraine* in 1945!

I beheld suddenly a fine wild landscape to the south. High rocky hills, as blue as sapphire, closed the view, and between these lay ridge upon ridge, heathery, craggy, the sun glittering on veins of rock.... The mists, which had hitherto beset me, were now broken into clouds.

Robert Louis Stevenson,
Travels with a Donkey in the Cévennes

Country Roads

A kind of glee creeps over me whenever I turn off a highway or main road. The map swarms with boondocks linked by *D*s, or *CD*s—*routes départementales*, minor roads, signaled in yellow on road signs. Getting lost in this enchanted labyrinth is a delight. Sooner or later, we retrieve the red of an *N*—a *nationale*—or the blue of an *A*—an *autoroute*. They too have their charms.

These roads, sometimes cambered or without curbs, simply sail through the countryside, idly undulating, swerving unexpectedly, crossing a wood offering some shade, skirting a pond where a gray heron hunts for dinner, or a tilled field in the shape of a woman's hip. Flowers sprout up among the grass in the verges: it's as bucolic as could be. Every fourth locality bears the name of a national or local saint. Thank heaven the houses around the main square aren't too modern; they reflect the personality of the *"pays"*—the "country," in the sense historian Fernand Braudel gives the term in his unforgettable study *The Identity of France*. Because none of the thousand or so *pays* comprising France resembles its neighbor. Passing through the Vexin to the Pays de Bray and then on to the Pays de Caux, you feel the difference within a few miles, without having left a Normandy where the green of the Pays d'Auge is quite different from that in the county of Ouche. There is literally a Green, a Black, and a White Périgord, and the nuance is as perceptible when one quits the Barrois for Lorraine, the Limousin Charente for that of Ruffec, the Boischaut for the Champagne of Berry, the Boulonnais for the Audomarois. The hills of the Sundgau are as unlike the rest of the Alsace as Millavois and the Larzac are unlike the plateaus surrounding Rodez or Saint-Affrique, or the massif of Monédières is unlike the plateau of Millevaches, to quote an example from Corrèze. Leaving Chalosse and crossing the Adour at Peyrehorade and climbing toward La Bastide-Clairence, everything changes, the shapes, the colors—you are in Basque Country.

Départementales and their local tributaries lead us through an unexplored, more voluptuous France. People think it is motionless, lifeless. Wrong: it is slow and understated, but it is far from down-in-the-mouth. It's hard to imagine its charms if one never leaves the fast, "red" roads. Especially since bypasses now circumvent the tiniest village.

Page 48
Landscape in the Périgord.

Facing page
"The *départementale* simply sails through the countryside, idly undulating, swerving unexpectedly, crossing a wood offering some shade." D. T.

Pages 52–53
Claude Sautet offers us a good dose of nostalgia in his movie *The Things of Life*, as Michel Piccoli and Romy Schneider lovingly explore this cinegenic *départementale*.

This France exists, however, I've seen it, I court her as a lover does a flame whom he always expects will surprise him. And she always does, as I never take the same road from A to B. Ever since I got my first moped, setting out in quest of new things to see on a *départementale* has been one of my abiding passions.

Away with Parisian prejudices! So-called "deepest, darkest" France, *"la France profonde"* does indeed slumber and then go downhill, if, without a city or a viable company in the vicinity, the young are driven into exile. They'd prefer not go. But village "cretinism" is no more common here than in Paris's Latin Quarter. As one leaves, one hesitates at a junction that nowadays almost inevitably takes the form of a roundabout. This type of inter-section has become so prevalent that the mayors may even be on the take. Still, one must count one's blessings if we are spared the "sculpture" of some local or regional "artist." It's best to follow the most minor road on offer: it is sure to be the most enchanting. A manor on a hilltop with a farm below, vineyards, a gentle slope, "a pocket of greenery through which babbles a river," in the words of Rimbaud. There's no risk of getting genuinely lost. In France side roads lead to a secondary that has to trundle down to a high-way, just as a tributary throws itself into a river or a slow train reaches a main line. As one wends one's way, one's experience of time becomes non-linear and one curses the council or the plan-ning authorities that stick up signposts either haphazardly or not at all. One swerves to avoid a deer or a hedgehog, slows down to gaze at a splendid herd of cows or a flock of mallards taking off. In the end, one would really like to lose oneself, the blue-black ribbon of the main road leads us back home soon enough.

> *If I had studièd*
> *At the time of my madcap youth,*
> *I would today have a house and soft bed*
> *Alas, I fled school*

These verses are by the fifteenth century outlaw poet François Villon. If I had *studièd* more methodically, instead of wandering down every country road on the map I unfolded and still unfold with a wholly physical desire, I may have forged myself a real career. But then I would have run after time. I have preferred to see it run like the sand in the hourglass, and I can have no regrets. Better still, I persevere because, as luck would have it, France's road network is one of the densest in the world, so my liking for the *départementale* can always be rekindled.

Deux Chevaux

With its cheeky frog's nose, its understatement and affability, the *"deux-deuche"* as the two-horsepower Citroën 2CV is known, was the symbol of improvised escapism at a time when France felt young again. It was not a car; it was a bosom buddy. Mine was secondhand, resprayed white, with dents all over. A present from my father, it was instrumental in making my studies last longer than they might, because it allowed me to regularly indulge my wanderlust, preferably in a couple or with a posse of my pals. It did not like motorways and emitted a consumptive wheeze when going up hills. The position of the gearshift made flirting problematic and the metal reinforcement under the front seats was scarcely more conducive. But how I doted on that old Rocinante! Old on paper and with some wounds, but temperamentally so youthful. While I was bluffing my way through my baccalaureate exams and then some kind of diploma, we remained inseparable; at the end, she knew France by heart. My France. Except for a handful of departments, we crossed the country from coast to coast, stopping in bars, churches, and stadiums. She would wait for me so sweetly, and, when I was drunk, she would drive us home. Or grind to a halt to let me doze. Before the 2CV, there'd been a Solex moped, then a Mobylette. After that, real cars made to get from A to B or to show off. Quite unlike my adorable *"deux-deuche,"* an accomplice on my frantic bids for escape. "Sky, love, liberty!"

The sole outlet for my emulation of Rimbaud was to fly along the strip of asphalt, far from the city, from college. If the sun shone, I'd push down the roof, the wind would swell my sails, and I'd wail that summer's number one. We were free, the car and me. In my memory, it is indistinguishable from those moments in life when the road stretches out unimpeded toward a dream of adventure. I felt like d'Artagnan; we'd just left Gascony and at the end of the lane I hoped to find three friends. It was a time when youth danced the twist into the future, hoping not to descend into adulthood too rapidly. The *"deux-deuche"* was not a grown-up like its big Citroën sisters, the DS and the ID, already married and settled down. She was fun and easygoing. With her lack of attitude, she resembled the type of girl I preferred, the life I desired to live, the France I liked to dream of.

Facing page
"A village church, a vicar in his cassock, a Deux Chevaux from the years of the twist. A retro image of backwoods France as captured by Cartier-Bresson in 1960." D. T.

Dordogne

Out there, among the tribe of the Arverni of Gaul, two brooks rubbed along together in the shadow of the volcanoes: the Dore and the Dogne. At the foot of the great stone cliffs of the Orgues de Bort, it's already a considerable river. For the locals, the dignity of the name of "river" asserted by the Garonne is unjustified, because the Dordogne marries its equal at the confluence of Bec d'Ambès, while the couple's offspring, the Gironde, disgorges into the ocean between two vineyards, the Médoc and the Côtes de Blaye. To the rear of the gorge overhanging my plateau, the Dordogne looks like a lake in Switzerland, but more austere: four hydroelectric dams have been erected here, the water submerging fishing villages as well as a Cistercian abbey. Rainstorms are frequent in these gullies; the wind howls, torrents overflow their bed. A romantic drama. At one time *gabarriers*, sailing broad-bellied barges called *gabarres*, would set off from the port of Spontour with their cargo of timber to sell at Libourne. The more intrepid pushed on to Bordeaux, while the far-sighted bought the marshy land at Pomerol or on the magic hill of Saint-Émilion. They became rich, some very rich, so that it is people from Corrèze who more or less rule the roost in the Libourne wine trade.

As a child I'd whittle boats out of fir-tree bark and launch them onto a brook that bounds down to the Dordogne. Destination: the Americas, in the trustworthy hands of this courier that linked us to Aquitaine and the Ocean. This is my river. There's not much elbow room until Argentat, where a bygone era of river traffic has bequeathed rows of fine medieval houses lining the banks. Granite and roofing stone. It was in Argentat that the journalist and historian Emmanuel Berl and his wife Mireille kept their heads down during the occupation after their (brief) fling with Marshal Pétain. And it is close to Argentat, in a pseudo-Gothic manor house at Saint-Chamant, that André Malraux joined a Resistance network in 1942. He camped there with Josette Clotis and their two children, an interlude in the Corrèze, which, interspersed by sorties with the Maquis guerrilla fighters, inspired pages in his *Antimémoires* that elevate the French Resistance to the heights of a Greek tragedy. A tragedy compounded by personal anguish, because Josette fell beneath the wheels of a local train in Saint-Chamant station and

Facing page
"At the foot of the Orgues de Bort, the Dordogne is already a considerable river." D. T.

Pages 58–59
"The first châteaux before Souillac... here the Dordogne begins to open up." D. T.
The château at Fayrac.

was killed. Malraux was already in Alsace and the tempo of events was accelerating. Nevertheless, he acquired leave to see his partner one last time, in a clinic in Tulle.

Waxing pink, sandstone and Roman tiles start at Beaulieu, where the gorge widens. It is best to take the D116 secondary road and follow the Dordogne on the left bank. It's as bucolic as you can get. The river reappears at the border with the Quercy, watering splendid towns that already have a Latin flavor: Carennac, Floirac. In places it is overhung by cliffs; somewhere around here stands the supposed site of Uxellodunum, where Caesar gained a great victory over the last stronghold of Gauls, proving his ferocity by cutting off the prisoners' hands. The past is another country.

The Dordogne snakes its way through Claysse and Saint-Osoy, near Martel. The first châteaux appear before Souillac, where it begins to open up. There are many on the uplands, as one approaches the Périgord; Fénelon's in verdant luxuriance and then that of the much-missed Josephine Baker hard by La Roque-Gageac and Beynac. This pair of ocher jewels, almost orange in the sunshine, literally clings to the cliff face. Best avoided in summer, when the valley teems with tourists joining forces with the resident English. It is true that the latter occupied Aquitaine for three centuries. After Bergerac, the riverbed broadens, while Aquitaine becomes less undulating and the Dordogne snakes toward Fleix and Sainte-Foy-la-Grande, Protestant outcrops in the radical-socialist lake that is Southwest France. It is salutary to pass through Castillon-la-Bataille, where the English got their come-uppance (in 1453, the year Constantinople was captured by the Turks). In Fronsac I find it hard to imagine that this river started where I hail from! Did my tiny bark boats really sail between these vines? Did they make it to Savannah or Charleston? I'd like to believe so.

The Dordogne's "invitation to the voyage" cannot be a mirage. As I follow its course I always have the impression of edging nearer the Holy Grail and at the spit at Graves I picture myself already on the other side of the Atlantic. I adore the Dordogne wherever it flows, but, to its charms in the Quercy and the Périgord, to its wifely languor when it reaches the estuary, I prefer its cloistered channel through gulches of granite awash with dark greenery, in Spontour or Chambon, with its trout streams and the ghosts of tiny ships.

Facing page
Beynac in Perigord: an ocher jewel, almost orange under the sun, it literally clings to the cliff.

To save Paris
is more than
to save France,
it is to save
the world.

Victor Hugo

French Writers

I hope that in this infatuated eulogy of France, a French writer may be permitted to quote from his fellow scribblers. No other country has allotted such prestige to its authors and foreign writers alike. However, this prestige has begun to dwindle. Still, our classics remain enthroned in the pantheon of well-read people the world over, and not so long ago the French used to honor their writers, be it for extra-literary reasons, as attested by the funerals of some of them: Hugo (delirious), Zola (moving), and Sartre (nostalgic). Three hundred thousand blubbing workers screaming *"Germinal"* in chorus before the coffin of a writer, Zola in this case: this is how closely French history used to be bound to its literary figures. They have divorced since, but still Nobel Prize-winning writers from both Europe and the Americas continue to come and ratify their status in the Latin Quarter, and several even feel the need to possess at least a pied-à-terre in Paris.

In no other country has the *terroir* spawned such a plethora of literary works as in France. Especially after France began to industrialize and the native cocoon metamorphosed into a vanished—or at least an endangered, forsaken, or degraded—Eden. Wherever I go in France, I am preceded or succeeded by a writer, and, inevitably, I can see his wanderings reflected in his writing. Hence the importance of Georges Simenon in my topographical journeys. He crisscrossed France in the 1920s and 1930s, before the cities, even the small ones, were engulfed by suburbs in a jumble of bypasses, social housing, industrial zones, and hypermarkets. I followed his tracks and certain places owe him all the poetry I found there.

Before Simenon there was Balzac, the great love of my twenties. I pursued him through Paris (at the bottom of rue Lhomond), to Issoudun, Limoges, Alençon, Arcis-sur-Aube, Sancerre, Guérande, in Touraine (Saché, Saumur, Saint-Cyr). I sought him near Angoulême, where he stayed with a certain Zulma Carraud, in a manor house on the banks of the Charente. After many misadventures on my Mobylette, down roads leading nowhere, at last a farmer pointed out Balzac's house. But it had belonged to the other one, Guez de Balzac, a letter writer of the time of the Musketeers.

I sought, tracked down, or ran into Chateaubriand in Brittany, the other Châteaubriant among the Brière peat bogs, Marcel

"Our classics remain enthroned in the pantheon of well-read people the world over and our towns all boast of having spawned the quill of at least one writer." D. T.

Page 62
Victor Hugo photographed by Paul Nadar in 1878.

Facing page
Portrait of Émile Zola painted by Manet in 1868, collection of the Musée d'Orsay in Paris.

Aymé in the Jura, Colette's childhood at Puisaye, joy according to Jacques Chardonne in Barbezieux, Bernanos's *country priest* in the Boulonnais, François Mauriac's adolescents in the Gironde moors, George Sand's *Petite Fadette* around La Châtre, André Dhôtel in the Ardennes, Maupassant in the Pays de Caux. In Aix, I muse tenderly about the pure, young heroine of Zola's *La Conquête de Plassans*, while, emerging from the cathedral at Saint-Omer, I can almost see those ladies in green hats satirized by Germaine Acremant in her 1920s potboiler *Ces dames aux chapeaux verts*. Manosque *is* Jean Giono; Guéret, Jouhandeau's Chaminadour, and, passing over the old bridge at Orthez on my way to Hasparren, my eye seeks out the donkeys of Francis Jammes. If I go to Burgundy to buy wine, I pass by Lamartine's hometown, Milly, where, as his poem alleges, *time suspends its flight*.

Major or minor, more or less regional in their material, all these writers gleaned crumbs of universality from the furrows of their region. I like to get my fill in situ. If one's reading precedes the journey, then one can turn the place into whatever one likes. Such bookish detours do not prevent me enjoying more earthly pleasures, and I rub shoulders as willingly with barmen as with local scholars. In the café, I enjoy diving into the local gazette to learn on the spot (that is, on the barstool) who's the district's MP, how people eke out a living, the division the soccer or rugby club plays in, to which metropolis the young go to study or to work, and on what line the rail station lies. But dining at Sancerre having read *La Muse du department* imparts added zip to your glass of Menetou-Salon served with a Crottin de Chavignol goat's cheese.

I owe French writers so much, the cult I dedicate to them is so childlike that I am not ashamed to track them down to their grave. On a pilgrimage to Rimbaud's last resting place I traveled by train to Charleville. Rimbaldisme is practically a religion for me. And not only for me: it was a weekday and pouring rain, yet the flowers deposed on his tomb looked fresh. I also saw a bunch on Charles Péguy's tomb in a field in the Brie inhabited by hopping rabbits. He died for France in 1914, just like Alain-Fournier.

The cemeteries of Paris are brimming with writers: Montmartre, Montparnasse, Passy, Père-Lachaise. Attempting to mitigate their loneliness, I have come to deplore their imprisonment. The tomb of Vigny, in the Montmartre cemetery bisected by rue Caulaincourt, gives onto a low-cost hotel. He did not deserve such an insult. Worse still, Zola exchanged the same cemetery for a cage in the

Facing page
"The France Proust resuscitates, invents, is a multifaceted one: there is of course his childhood.... But then there is that '*doulce France*,' which percolates up from the most distant past." D. T.
Here, Proust's bedroom as reconstituted in Illiers-Combray.

Facing page
"The importance
of Simenon in my
topographical journeys.
He crisscrossed France
in the 1920s and
1930s.... I followed his
tracks and certain places
owe him all the poetry I
found there." D. T.

Panthéon. A similar mishap occurred to Dumas, who was perfectly at home in Villers-Cotterêts, the city of Francis I's famous edict. Sand almost suffered the same fate, as her admirers were determined to see her in the Panthéon. She is much better off in the little cemetery at Nohant, next to the chapel, behind her own house. I hope and pray she stays there. God preserve writers from politicians! Georges Bernanos is fine in Pellevoisin, Paul Valéry perched up in his *cimetière marin* at Sète, Chateaubriand on his rock at Saint-Malo, Tocqueville just behind the church in the village that bears his name. François Mauriac pulled the short straw: Vémars lies at the end of a runway at Roissy. One misjudged takeoff and a Boeing might crash-land on his august remains. He would have been better off buried in Malagar, where trains rumble over the bridge spanning the Garonne.

Thanks be to the muses, the majority of my favorite writers have escaped the Panthéon: Rutebeuf, François Villon, all the greats of the Renaissance and of the Grand Siècle, Marivaux, Casanova, André Chénier, Balzac, Alfred de Vigny, Alfred de Musset, Lamartine, Baudelaire, Rimbaud, Verlaine, Proust, Mallarmé, Francis Jammes, Henri Bergson, Herny de Montherlant, Camus, Cioran, and even François Mauriac. The only ones to have swallowed the bait were Hugo (he asked for it), Zola, Dumas (political reasons), and André Malraux, who might perhaps have appreciated it.

I unblushingly acknowledge a predilection for the writers of my own country. This has not prevented me from looking elsewhere; it's my penchant for distant climes. However, a La Fontaine fable, a tirade from *Le Cid*, or certain verses from Hugo's *Feuilles d'automne* will always affect me more than even the most beautiful passages in foreign literature. The Renaissance poet du Bellay writes of his preference for the "abode built by his ancestors" to any other: this also applies to the flush of desire I feel whenever I take down a volume from the "Pléiade" collection in my library. But why not escape and read a foreign author? I hesitate but always end up choosing a French author, in the knowledge that this escape will lead my heart back to its true source.

I am not aware of a single week since my adolescence without my reading a French writer; nor a year without rereading a few of our great classics. When I am writing a book, I read only our greatest stylists—from Jean de La Bruyère to Paul Morand—in the perhaps vain hope that my pen will not be deemed too unworthy of their excellence.

Fashion fades;
only style remains
the same.

Coco Chanel

Fabulous La Fontaine

A master crow, perched on a tree one day,
Was holding in his beak a piece of cheese.
A master fox....

Generations of French schoolchildren have recited the *Fables* of
La Fontaine, without always comprehending in what way the
chatter equates to the *matter*. These tales, with their argumen-
tative little animals afflicted with human passions, provided an
access to French culture in an age when well-born children from
Saint Petersburg to Vienna were required to learn the language. A
classic introduction to the genius of the *grand siècle*, though with
none of its coldness, they revive the joys of spring of that imposing period. La Fontaine's bestiary offers enchantment to every age,
like Charles Perrault's *Mother Goose Tales*. The magnanimous
lion, the fly on the coach axle, the greenhorn mouselet, the sly-
boots fox, the sweet but dumb bear, the heron with a long bill
sheathed in a still longer neck, the rat hiding in a round of Dutch
cheese: the pictures fly by.

But, better than that, in each one can be discerned a contemporary of our own. Who can say they have never met a cat, or something else, like Raminagrobis, "nicely rounded, fat, and fatty,"
and as hypocritical as the day is long? The human characters are
no less recognizable: Perrette and her pot of milk epitomizes those
pipe dreamers who, without a penny to their name, build castles
in the air. The morals were nevertheless always pretty clear: a dog
may be well fed and better lodged, but a wolf conserves his freedom. The analogy with what I had to endure in the classroom or
even at home was also pretty clear. Their air of lightness and the
sayings in the prologue or epilogue to each fable lay the foundations of a morality at once Christian, epicurean, and stoic, with
more than a dash of common sense and disillusioned compassion
for mankind. The French employ expressions from the *Fables* vir-
tually every day.

As an adult, I have reread the *Fables* countless times. I revel
in their poetry ("The waters were as transparent as in the finest
days"), in their scarcely veiled irony, barbs of cynicism, and word-
play, and I admire how, out of the flimsiest material—Aesop's

Page 70
French charm and
elegance: an ad from
the 1940s by the famous
poster artist René Gruau
for "Rouge Baiser."

Facing page
"There is, I see, no
coward on earth /
Who cannot find more
cowardly than he."
"The Hare and the
Frogs," illustrated
by Gustave Doré.

Greek *Fables*, essentially—his debonair quill has chiseled such exquisite jewels. What could be more original! What could be more French! It is flowing, lighthearted, musical: it runs as from a living, clear spring. His licentious verses add to his lyric palette a more lubricious vein of which he later repented (though how sincerely remains uncertain) so as Louis XIV would agree "to consummate" his election to the French Academy.

This indolent, inconsistent, but heavenly idler could do anything with words, but his *Fables* exceed all else he did. He lived through his time, or floated by it as heedlessly as the unthinking grasshopper. Perhaps indifferent, undoubtedly lazy, certainly lacking concentration. This vaguely ennobled member of the gentry with an anarchic side sought to cure a financier's insomnia with the songs of a cobbler ("The Cobbler and the Financier").

Pedagogy has moved on since then; various Republics have supplanted the kings of yore and rote-learning has long been off-limits. Teachers continue, however, to make schoolkids recite these sad, funny, or cruel stories—of a lion helped by a rat, of a goat ensnared by a fox, of a weasel impudently squatting a rabbit's abode, of a *parvenu* frog swelling up and up. It is as if primary schools were reluctant to sever the last thread linking the culture known as "humanist" to the newer, TV-based upstart. But until when?

"A certain fox from Gascony, others say from Normandy." I know by heart more lines by La Fontaine than by any other poet, and all gleaned from his *Fables*. Crafted in a language at the high summer of its maturity, aided and abetted by a boyish cheek, the lessons of this bestiary remain a miraculous episode in the history of French literature. They offer the best way into the *grand siècle*, into its baroque and classicism, but they go further than that: they attain the realm of fairyland.

Le Corbeau et Le Renard

The Frenchwoman

Her tenderness is prone to sudden eclipse and her aversions can sometimes seem overlong. But a Frenchwoman is always by far the most elegant. The most concerned with her appearance, until the grave. And the most attentive to the whisperings of her looking glass. Whether she is moneyed or broke, whether she adopts a preppy style or something more street, she adores clothes. And make-up. And perfume.

Practically all the legendary couturiers have been French. Coco Chanel even made her entrance into literature through the pages of the novelist Michel Déon. Almost all the most prestigious beauty brands are French too. And, if a suitor presents his belle with a diamond from Bulgari or from Van Cleef & Arpels, it is even more opulent if it comes in packaging from a store on place Vendôme. This increasingly democratized taste for luxury has modeled, designed, and adorned French women. During the occupation many women scarcely had enough food to eat. In any other country they would have devoted all their energies to ensuring supplies and keeping out of harm's way. All while doing this, Frenchwomen also sought ways of remaining attractive, be it with tat or hand-me-downs, even drawing ersatz stocking seams in pencil down their calves. Our grandmas, even our great-grandmas, come up with tricks attesting to their dress sense. A brooch, a necklace, a shawl: with these deceptively understated additions that make all the difference, an old lady shows she has something more than her bearing, her dignity, or her opulence.

In fact, the Frenchwoman is a reflection of our literature and our philosophy. An ambiguous one, since she seems forever split between a thirst for head-over-the-heels happiness and a curious amalgam of narcissism and puritanism in the manner she deals with her emotions.

Facing page
Brigitte Bardot, who sat for the bust of Marianne, is a French icon, the symbol of 1960s France. She poses here rolled up in a tricolor flag in the studio of Sam Levin, who immortalized her in several photographs.

Pages 78–79
"A Frenchwoman is always by far the most elegant." D. T. Ines de la Fressange photographed in the apartment of Coco Chanel, is an undeniable icon of French elegance.

An hour is
not merely
an hour, it is
a vase full
of scents
and sounds
and projects
and climates.

Marcel Proust,
Time Regained

Train Stations

In the nineteenth century, train stations sprouted up all over France like daisies in a field. They can be found in places out in the sticks with no claim to fame. Six Paris stations connect the major provincial cities to the borders and shores of the mainland. This centralized policy also governs our road network and airline routes. It dates back to our kings, was taken up by the Jacobins and Napoleon, while Third Republic radical-socialists also added their two cents. If one has the nose for it, in the vicinity of the six main stations one can get a whiff of the region they serve: the street names, the look of the passengers, the waiters' accents in nearby hotels and restaurants. Auvergnats have proliferated around Austerlitz, Bretons in Montparnasse, and if you lunch at Le Train Bleu in the Gare de Lyon or opposite at L'Européen, you can tell that people are about to head southwards. In the Terminus Nord one is already in Calais, practically in England.

I have often succumbed to these "invitations to the voyage." I am intimately acquainted with all the brasseries in every station in Paris and I lament the demise of the one in Montparnasse, ousted by a nondescript carbuncle of irremediable ugliness. I also regret not having known the Gare d'Orsay at the time Mauriac's Thérèse Desqueyroux arrived there in her quest for a freedom to be gained only in the air of Paris. At least that's what provincials believe when their overheated minds buzz round and round in their hometown, like a wasp in a bottle. You can read this on the faces of new arrivals: a longing ripened by languishing under a stone out in the sticks. Such cravings, though, are not incompatible with a certain angst. People who return to the "country" for the weekend, the vacations, or forever look less flustered than an ambitious, covetous, "Rastignac" type. In the provinces-to-Paris direction, pipe dreams are a solitary affair, and nobody addresses a word to their neighbor. In the opposite direction, tongues are looser.

I love our trains and their stations. They reign over a kind of railroad civilization. In France, trains too inspire poetry. I like to take one from a Paris station in the early afternoon. At first it's always crammed. The first stops. Passengers get off but almost no one gets on. A change. You climb into a local train whose tapering nose resembles that of a TGV, which in the end deposits you

Page 80
"I regret not having known the Gare d'Orsay." D. T. The huge clock still adorns the canopy of this station that became a museum in 1986.

Facing page
A wonder of railway architecture, the Byzantine-style station of Limoges, inaugurated in 1929, with its large dome surmounted by a minaret and its clock tower measuring 187 feet (57 meters) high.

Pages 84–85
"I love our trains and their stations." D. T. Claude Monet shared this fascination: he devoted twelve canvases to the Gare Saint-Lazare, the symbol of the nascent industrial revolution.

in some mid-ranking town, or a village, sometimes not even that. Night has long fallen. Nobody on the station forecourt. Hangars, some houses, and, on the corner of the avenue, a drab neon sign reads, "Hôtel de la Gare." Dreams come and go, and come back again from the heart to its most far-flung capillaries. You push open the door. On the wall ads for an aperitif and a photo of the local soccer team. Ricard ashtrays on Formica tables. The somnolent proprietor is absorbed in reading the sports' or obituary pages of the local rag. The last train is long gone. In the yellow glow from the streetlamps, the deserted platform looks to have given up the ghost. In the distance, a reddish gleam struggles for life in the fog. The station has dozed off. If the fog ever lifts, you'll discern the indistinct forms of this godforsaken place. It too is asleep. There is something remorseless about the night in these country towns of no great account. The hotel looks like a rickety lighthouse.

A bell rings out thinly. A goods train passes dead slow. Reassuring, moving, and disturbing all at once. A low rumble, two red lights and then night, black as pitch. This is a certain France. Night gathering around a station far from civilization, destined to disappear because economists deem it surplus to requirements. They have their reasons. Mine are poetic. I often find myself scribbling doggerel in such places while in a five-star hotel my pen dries up. Day breaks. Rain, fog. A shower with a will of its own. Dishwater coffee, croissants that have seen better days. Who cares? The trains stop, the station comes to life. It's time to explore your surroundings.

This has often happened to me, and normally the town has ended up being worth the detour. Thousands of French towns are "worth the detour," at least once, and one regret I will take with me to the grave is that I haven't got to know all of them.

In the early afternoon you climb into the local train plying in the opposite direction. As on the way down, you need to change, and you clamber aboard the fast train bound for Paris. This time people pour on at every stop, but nobody gets off. Night falls on the Beauce or the Brie or Picardy. Then Paris.

I have an almost visceral need for these comings-and-goings on the train, as if between two facets of the French soul. It reflects our dual citizenship based on the land. Scratch a card-carrying Parisian—a boy from the hood, or a moneyed one with a view over the Seine—and you'll find the blood of a true-blue provincial. I often spot them at the Gare d'Austerlitz, humming with impatience, with, in one special corner of their heart, a church tower.

A French Feast

In the land of winegrowing monks and Rabelaisian greed the Michelin Guide stirs up a hornet's nest each time it decrees its stars, and it's scarcely an exaggeration to say some recipes are discovered only at the opening of the will. They are only passed on to the most intimate circle, though not without first expiating until the cows come home about how one just *has* to put a vanilla pod in with the peach jam. Or on the exact proportion of chocolate in the sauce for hare à la royale. In France, food is a religion with its own canon law, its theologians (Brillat-Savarin), its reformers, heretics, liturgy, and nomenclature. A dish has to simmer long in the French imagination before it can be smelled, contemplated, tasted. Ingredient or recipe, the name evokes the land from where it came, or, failing that, a mark of authenticity as to its production. When the suggestion is tripe à la mode de Caen, sole à la dieppoise, Castelnaudary cassoulet, pig's trotters à la Sainte-Menehould, ham à la jovinienne, pages from the colored album of French cultural diversity pass before our salivating eyes. Our taste buds put much store in roots: andouille must come from Vire, chili pepper from Espelette, poularde from Bresse, cooked sausage with potatoes sautéed in oil from Lyon, quiche from the Lorraine, pork hotpot from the Limousin, potted-meat rillettes from Le Mans. There is no *aligot* or *truffade* worth its salt to be had outside the Auvergne and authentic bouillabaisse is confined to the area around Notre-Dame-de-la-Garde. Alsace deals in poussin with Riesling, the Bourbonnais in pompe brioche with crackling, the Berry in coq au vin, the Corrèze in milk-fed calf's-head, and oysters must sail in from Marennes with the tide. For mussels *mouclade* one has to travel to La Rochelle, while the smoked pork sausage, the Jésus de Morteau, must come from Morteau. Check the "Appellation d'Origine" label, as for our wines and cheeses. It would be a huge blunder to order Livarot cheese in Roquefort, Nice's pissaladière in Lille, or a glass of Buzet in Chablis.

As a blue-blooded Frenchman, I like to eat and drink. The geography of our culinary traditions is not without links to our literature. I like recipes with a marked accent and a swagger. I confess a weakness for those that increase the cholesterol level (stews, salamis, daubes, confits, offal) and a penchant for feathered game: partridge cooked in cabbage or woodcock served on a canapé of minced offal.

Facing page
"A dish has to simmer long in the French imagination before it can be smelled, contemplated, tasted."
D. T.

Pages 88–89
"As a blue-blooded Frenchman, I like to eat and drink.... I owe so much to so many chefs."
D. T.
Paul Bocuse, photographed by Marc Riboud in 1975.

My national fervor revels in what outsiders find repugnant: snails (in Burgundy, Charentais, or Bordeaux styles), frog legs (with tomatoes, à la provençale), elver with lashings of garlic, crunchy pig's tail and pig's ear, bunting that melts beneath the tongue. As a starter, rabbit hearts washed down with Pouilly Fumé suit me well—a discovery I owe to the onetime proprietor of L'Espérance.

I owe so much to so many chefs, not counting my wife, impeccable on calf sweetbreads with cèpes, shoulder of lamb, stuffed cabbage, and *farcidure* "dumplings," a Corrèze specialty. My mother is peerless when it comes to chicken in cream, quiche, and meat pâtés. I have gastronomized throughout France, in innumerable greasy spoons and sometimes in award-winning restaurants, although their exorbitance and sophistication put me off. Being neither a specialist nor a fundamentalist I prefer unfussy inns where a grumpy owner serves up deviled eggs, omelet with chanterelle mushrooms, andouillette sausage and chips, trout with almonds, veal chop *forestière*, black pudding with apple, a real gudgeon fry-up, or dandelion salad with bacon pieces. It all resides in the cook's skill and French cooks almost have the knack of yesteryear's homely housewives. Disappointment only ensues when they try to blind one with science in an effort to obtain a star, a fork, or some other award.

I am anything but xenophobic and I relish the taste of Italian, Chinese, and Arabic cuisine, some being of unimpeachable refinement. But, in the end, and without taking sides, none can compare with French. Only in France do they know how to rustle up something that can dissolve beneath the tongue so poetically. Nowhere else does food enflame the lyric muse and exacerbate the passions. No other possesses such an abundant literature devoted to things gourmet, since Brillat-Savarin's *Philosopher in the Kitchen* to Pierre Benoit's fantastical *Déjeuner de Sousceyrac*. I must have devoured that novel ten times and I've lunched in Sousceyrac to see its setting for myself. It is only in France that the eye brightens eagerly as it peruses the menu, before being further gladdened by the appearance of a well-stocked cheese trolley.

In France every product has a soul that I like to catch sight of in the early morning at the Rungis market, with all the colors, scents, and traders' slang. I go there for an imaginary journey through the French *"pays"* and every time it's like revisiting a scene from Zola's *Belly of Paris*. I also like window-shopping at a pork-butcher's stall. What could be more sensual than a line of swinging hams, a regiment of hocks in breadcrumb, an assortment of *saucissons* cooked in garlic or dried in ash, long thin ones and ovoids alike? Andou-illes sheathed in black, terrines, brawn and head cheese, liver pâté, pots of rillettes with crackling, feet in breadcrumbs, headcheese and parsley, *cervelas*, pale-pink pork chops, flitches of bacon—they all send me into seventh heaven. I've noticed too how charcuterie butchers are always merry. Nowhere else but in France can one find such an allegory of abundance combined with the joy of a good blowout. Here, epicureanism exalts food, endowing happiness with an aesthetic dimension. It is under this flag that our elite chefs travel the world offering cooking courses and accreditation.

I have countless memories of eating out—in Paris, in the prov-inces—returning more than once if it's good. Still, I never tire of hunting down new eateries to which I might whistle over a team of buddies. We tend to sit at the back so we can talk as loudly and laugh as indecorously as we desire. I choose homemade dishes that cleave to the body and wines that still speak patois. An adept of heavy-duty gastronomy, I inevitably have reservations about "nou-velle cuisine." There are exceptions—in particular Guy Savoy, who can lighten a recipe without making it bland, and who concocts wonders without overdoing it. Perhaps because he loves and plays rugby, and because he has never severed his ties with his native Isère. Moreover, the excesses of culinary purification, which can be laid at the door of dietary moralizing, are beginning to flag: the "moderns" have gone back to sauces, while the "old hands" now lay them on less thickly. And so, in spite of the proliferation of McDonald's that our offspring find so irresistible, the land of Rabelais remains a paradise for the taste buds.

La Tupina. This is my favorite restaurant. I've liked others in France, and even in Bordeaux (especially Ramet), but this one pres-ents a perfect allegory of my ideal eatery. You open the door to a vast fireplace burning a wood fire over which roast poultry or shoulders of lamb. Corn-fed yellow chicken from Saint-Sever, Pauillac lamb. Everything depends on the authenticity of the produce: this is how chef Xiradakis plotted, and won, his thirty years' war against "nou-velle cuisine." Henceforth, "Xira" is considered a lord of Bordeaux and caters for the local gentry and passing celebrities alike. When I first came across him, he wasn't trendy. In those days much time was wasted in up-market restaurants deciphering menus that seemed to have been lifted from *Finnegans Wake*. The plates looked like Miró drawings, the steamed contents accompanied by a plethora of aromas so sophisticated that one's taste buds went round in circles.

Good food and good wine,
these are heaven on earth.

Henry IV

Henry IV

Prior to its five republics, two empires, and occasional interregnum best forgotten, France was ruled by kings. Great kings, upstanding ones, poor ones, plain bad ones, as well as certified lunatics. The most popular is also my favorite. We venerate Saint Louis, we admire Louis XIV (or not), and we feel sorry for Louis XVI (or not). But the French love Henry IV. In fact, his legend only dates back to the historians of the Third Republic and in his lifetime he had quite a few enemies, even after the abjuration of Protestantism at Saint-Denis, the coronation at Chartres, and his triumphant entrance into Paris. There were several attempts on his life before he was assassinated by Ravaillac and Protestant extremists detested him as much as the Catholic League. For the French—for me—the memory of "good king Henry", sagely advised by the "good" Sully, still burns bright. The image of a wiseacre from Gascony, neither haughty nor cruel, and certainly not sectarian (his Edict of Nantes granted Protestants rights in Catholic France). A quarrelsome gambler with protruding chin and neat beard, his breath reeked of garlic. An inveterate philanderer who bedded maidservants and duchesses alike.

During the partisan wars, Henry and his merry band cavorted through a kingdom that was not yet his. It is tempting to suppose that he sowed his wild oats far and wide: his way of honoring a place. A plaque recalls his passage on the bridge at Argentat at the bottom of my native plateau. If one extrapolates, the blood of the Bourbons and the kings of Navarre runs, at least symbolically, through the veins of every Frenchman: he has ennobled us all.

The white plume, the eternally skirt-chasing "Vert-Galant," his "Paris is well worth a Mass," Givry (his favorite wine), Ravaillac: out of this history and mythology the collective imagination concocts a king without a capital "K"—truculent, jovial, attractive. As indeed he was—if, on occasion, also untrustworthy and underhand. Fiery in combat, prudent and patient in his conquest of the crown, he had an intuition of not only the true meaning of legitimacy but also of the significance of minorities. Up to a point, all our greatest politicians, from Richelieu to de Gaulle, as they strove to govern against extremists of every stripe and grandees of every hue, take their cue from his pragmatism.

Page 92
Henry IV on his white horse. Seventeenth-century stained glass in the castle at Pau.

Facing page
Portrait of "Good King Henry" by Frans Pourbus (1610): "A truculent king and a bon vivant." D. T.

955

My garden is my most beautiful masterpiece.

Claude Monet

The Impressionists

The impressionists rediscovered, re-enchanted the world.

Everything after stems from them: fauvism, cubism, expression-ism, abstract art. They are the one great pictorial school of our modern times, a dazzling adventure, the only true French episode after centuries of Italian and then Flemish supremacy. The move-ment was also the most successful illegitimate scion of the French bourgeoisie in its rudest health, in spite of Sedan and the Commune. It benefited from some first-rate tutors: the romantics (especially Delacroix), Corot, Courbet, the second School of Fontainebleau and that of Barbizon. And, once the impressionists had imposed their dazzling vision of light, Proust translated it into verbal volutes and Debussy into sound. It well and truly was a "revolution," if we go back to the etymology of the word and ignore all the romantic claptrap of the "artist accursed." Moreover our magicians did not spend that long "accursed." The middle-classes, from which they almost all came, quickly adopted, promoted, financed, and feted them. Seldom can dissidence have so rapidly become adopted as the norm. Clemenceau, who was no harum-scarum, wrote a book on Monet, who in turn painted his portrait. What an irony of his-tory: so terrified of revolution, the French bourgeoisie nonetheless bequeathed to the world one of the most radical ones imaginable. The impressionists created the "new man"—the ideologues' platitu-dinous fantasy—peaceably, and as it were in passing.

Their story is common knowledge. No school has been so amply dissected, though it remains unclear in what category Van Gogh, Cézanne, or Gauguin should be placed. In impressionism's open house, each composes their bouquet with flowers from their own secret garden. I am fascinated by Monet's *Water Lilies*—both the ones in the Musée Marmottan in Paris and the enormous canvas in the newly built museum in Basel. My way of admiring a tym-panum on a Gothic cathedral owes a great deal to that in Rouen, as painted by Monet. I adore the landscapes along the banks of the Seine by Pissarro and Sisley, Renoir's female sitters, Degas's danc-ers and horses. I love them all, from Manet and Berthe Morisot to their successors: Vuillard, Bonnard, Van Dongen, Vallotton. It is to follow in their footsteps that I travel to Étretat, Honfleur, or Trouville. They made the Normandy seashore seem enchanted,

Page 96
"I am fascinated by Monet's *Water Lilies*, the ones in the Musée Marmottan." D. T.

Facing page
"Trouville, where I like to walk along the boardwalk as far as the Roches Noires." D. T. Painting by Claude Monet (1870), Musée d'Orsay.

Right
"They made the train
stations, the bridges
seem enchanted." D. T.
The Boieldieu Bridge
at Rouen, painted by
Pissarro in 1896.

proceeding to do as much for the train stations, the bridges, the barges, the Grand Boulevards, and the Butte Montmartre. They cleansed with their poetry a world that the industrial era had rendered ugly, offering, free to all who can see, the secret truth behind a marvelous journey. Theirs. And now it is ours. It all seems miraculous. It is a blessing that has earned France immense prestige among all peoples and in every milieu.

Since a taste for "classical" painting implies a mythological, biblical, and historical culture, as well as a reasonable familiarity with art history, the layman can feel left out. At best he admires, unmoved. And the same might be said for so-called "modern" art. The emotion of your average tourist in front of an impressionist picture, however, is never fake. By the grace of these miracle-workers, his eye foments his own, unconscious "revolution." A woman's smile, a quivering leaf, the flight of a passing butterfly, a patch of sun on the grass. It all appears before my eye and engulfs me, moment by moment, and I absorb it with an impressionist tremor of what is called interiority.

Impressionism: the mere word evokes a dazzling frisson of the soul that can weave threads of reality into a kind of ecstasy.

Facing page
"I love all the impressionists, as well as their successors: Vuillard, Bonnard, Vallotton." D. T. *Nude in Backlighting*, painted by Pierre Bonnard in 1908.

In the mirror of his pond, among the heavy flagstones
of watery foliage encircled by clouds, there surges
an explosion of petals enthralled by the meandering haze
from which the flame of water or the splendor
of heavenly appeasement in turn upwells. It is here that
Monet came to seek the refinement of his acutest sensations.

Georges Clemenceau, *Claude Monet*

Claude Monet on the Japanese bridge
overlooking the water-lily pond in his garden at Giverny.

Whatever thing
men call great,
look for it
in Joan of Arc,
and there
you will find it.

Mark Twain

Joan of Arc

In the heart of her history, France was gifted with a flesh and blood Antigone. She ennobles it and such a privilege is inestimable. Joan belongs to legend and the Church, belatedly, canonized her. But this saint really existed and came from the Arc family in the land of the Barrois, where she watched over the sheep and heard voices. The flight to Vaucouleurs is no fable, no more than the conversation at Chinon with poor Charles VII in winter 1429. Her boldness was so intrepid that, in Poitiers, after vetting her thoroughly, the "king of Bourges" presented her with a panoply of weapons. Her voices? Their message is very plain: God ordained two distinct kingdoms, each to their own territory, and in the land of France just one legitimate king, Charles VII. Yield to this inevitability and the peace of the Lord will be upon all. What could be more splendid than an armed virgin surging out from Blois toward Orléans as spring breaks singing "Veni Creator Spiritus!" What could be more miraculous than her triumph over Talbot! Nobody believed in her—neither the king nor his shifty politicians, who already loathed her. Politicians always hate heroes and saints: even if they dive under their skirts whenever terror seizes them. The battles of Jargeau, Beaugency, Patay. A fantastic cavalcade on the road to the political Holy Grail whose necessity Joan had instinctively grasped: the anointment of Charles VII at Reims to put an end to disputes about legitimacy.

For the calamitous, then tragic events that ensued, politicians were responsible. Behind Joan's back they wheeled and dealed, and so there followed the retreat before Paris, the failure at La Charité, and her capture at Compiègne. The Burgundians, the English, the University of Paris, the archbishop of Winchester: all bit-parts in a plot designed to extinguish the stars in heaven that her innocence had set ablaze. In the words of Charles Péguy, whose verses glorify the finest, purest, and noblest heroine in France's history, it was the vengeance of the politician on the mystic. The trial confirmed her sainthood and her martyrdom consecrated it. France owes Joan's brief incursion into the field of politics, diplomacy, and warfare a great deal. As the country was saved by Antigone, all Creons were placed under advisement. Because Joan, before her martyrdom, had triumphed, France will be, and for all time, more than France.

Page 106
"What remains of the redemptive innocence of Joan of Arc." D. T. Here J. E. Millais paints her listening to the voices telling her to march on Orléans.

Facing page
"What could be more splendid than an armed virgin surging out from Blois toward Orléans." D. T.
In this painting by Jean-Jacques Scherrer she makes her entry into Orléans after having forced the English to lift their siege.

From floor to floor,
as the king of France went
up the marvelous staircase
of his château of Blois,
he could see the broad
expanse of the beautiful
Loire, which brought him
news of all his kingdom.

Honoré de Balzac

Brasserie Lipp

The *père* Cazes, with his mustache and cigar, is no longer there, but his spirit continues to oversee the ceremonial of being directed to a table in conformity with the unbending rules of an unspoken protocol. On the ground floor, needless to say. Upstairs is for tourists. They climb the spiral staircase and rubberneck for the new starlet on the block, a recent tennis champion, a defense attorney to the wayward glitterati, a minister with a lady friend, an American producer lending a doubting ear to a highbrow novelist's "idea." Out-of-towers may also be shoved under the awning, as if for sale in a shopwindow. Or in the room at the back: the "purgatory."

Nobody comes to Lipp to eat, though the food is excellent. I have a weakness for the stuffed pig's trotters, knuckle of veal with lentils, pistachio-encrusted paté, *cervelas remoulade*. Neither do you come to drink the place dry, although a carafe of Côte de Brouilly and the draft brown ale go down nicely.

Some go to Lipp to be seen. Others to have a closer look at those who go there to be seen. The former arrange matters so they sit on a bench against the wall, close to the cash desk by the radiator. The latter swing round like weathercocks every time anyone comes in.

Habitués breeze in through the revolving door and take a table as if at home, but in an art nouveau decor. The frescoes on the brownish ceiling host nudes cavorting among pink birds. The same exotic taste transpires in the pale-green tiles adorning the walls between two mirrors: a floral pattern with banana leaves and cockatoos. Don't trust the clock; it's always fast. The discreet but fulsome attentions of personnel better informed as to the arcana of Parisian life than any gazeteer add to the experience.

Many literary prizes are awarded in cafés: at Lipp (Prix Cazes), at the Flore, the Deux Magots. The chattering classes—not all as bookish as they make out—sit there inventing some new "ism" or other, or dreaming up ways of changing the world. Whenever I leave Lipp, unsteadily if after last orders with a regular or two kind enough to put up with this clodhopping country lad, my eye wanders toward the bell tower of the church of Saint-Germain-des-Prés. Lipp, that honey-pot for celebrities from the world over since the 1920s, has managed to keep a provincial soul in the beating heart of "parisianisme." This is the secret of its free and easy manner.

Page 110
The famous staircase at the Château de Blois in a nineteenth-century engraving.

Facing page
"Habitués breeze in through the revolving door and take a table as if at home, but in an art nouveau decor." D. T.

The Loire

Even if our national pride had no other claim to eternal fame, the reigns of the Valois have scattered enough châteaux down the Loire Valley to justify it tenfold. I know dozens of them. On each new excursion, I discover new ones, though I never forget to reacquaint myself with the most famous: Chambord, Azay, Chenonceau, Valençay, Villesavin, Ussé, and Cheverny, the inspiration behind Marlinspike Hall in *Tintin*. Almost all have medieval portions, revamped during the Renaissance in keeping with the fashion brought in from Italy. Borrowed, not imitated: the Loire châteaux attest to an authentic French genius. The land between Blois and Saumur is almost as familiar to me as my own village.

I like to gaze across at Blois from its surrounds: spires, dome, gray roofs like lacework. To the right, just as in Nevers, the modern age has seen fit to erect a concrete monstrosity. At a snail's pace the river, light chestnut in color, heaves against the cutwaters. I have always thought that a girlfriend kissed me on this very bridge, but I might be mistaken. I have walked through this town, with its castle in three styles, so often and have pictured the (convenient) assassination of Henri de Guise in my mind's eye so frequently, it is as if I witnessed it with Henry III and his mother.

One day, I spoke with President Chirac from a phone booth at the foot of the castle. I remember feeling sorry for him. He was caught up in some deadly dull business in his presidential palace, while I was reveling in French history, fancy-free. To each his fate.

At Chaumont, to see this picture I have always imagined painted by Nicolas de Staël, one has to approach it from the right bank: the village slumbers below, a long streak of white, and the château in its park is viewed from its good side, from the court. Chaumont is the one in which I would most liked to have lived. Catherine de' Medici let Diane de Poitiers have it after the death of Henry II as a consolation prize for grabbing Chenonceau. She was not amused.

The history of France was also played out in Amboise, as in Blois: kings, queens, and princes, feasts and assassinations. Long ago I stayed in a chalky house overhanging the Clos-Lucé. I know the city well, it is almost too pretty to be true. Very early troglodyte dwellings. Balzac at Vouvray (*L'Illustre Gaudissart*). He will stay with me until Guérande (*Béatrix*). Tours has got too big. You

get lost on the bypass between the industrial zone and a wasteland, before stumbling across the vestiges of the Château de Plessis, since converted into a "Drama Outreach Center." A sorry end for the *manes* of Louis XI, Charles VIII, Anne of Brittany, and Louis XII. And yet Pierre de Ronsard ended his days in the nearby ruins of the old abbey of Saint-Cosme. One can visit his house and his grave. A verse or two floats into the memory. Ronsard and du Bellay: French grace at its most lyrically bucolic—and erotic. Two words that rhyme perfectly, and that already rhymed long ago when I spent my time searching for shreds of Balzac's universe. I had found *Le Curé de Tours* around the cathedral of Saint-Gatien where Saint Martin was crowned bishop and where the children of Charles VIII and Anne of Brittany repose. Then *La Grenadière* at Saint-Cyr, a town whose mayor happens to be a friend.

Right bank. Luynes is a medieval castle—harsh, gloomy, virile. When writing a book about the Duchess of Chevreuse, I was shown around by the since deceased duke accompanied by the Count of Luynes! Nothing remains of Cinq-Mars. Razed to the ground by Richelieu. The Cardinal did not approve of the great and the good cooping themselves up in fortresses. Were he in power today, I bet he would demolish the "authorities" of every department and region—those modern duchies. I feel for Cinq-Mars, beheaded on the orders of the very same Richelieu. He was looking for trouble, but he was only twenty-two. The gigantic towers of the Château de Langeais look like a bear's forepaws above the gray roofs of the little town. That's Balzac again (*La Duchesse de Langeais*).

You cross through the Bourgueil vineyard and return to the river skirted by a road over a dam. The Loire is in its full majesty. The neat little houses below are built of cream-colored tufa. If you leave the highway you discover on a country road a discreetly elegant manor in red and black polychrome brick, half-fifteenth and half-seventeenth century: it belonged to Gédéon Tallemant des Réaux, whose amusing and scandalous *Historiettes* of court life are so piquant. Did he compose them in this oasis? I'd like to think so. I also like to picture Marie, Dumas's heroine, waiting for me in the Château de Montsoreau. It is so romantic, with its facade gazing down over the Loire. Alas! They stage "cultural events" there. The spell is broken. You're better off pacing the village streets, watching the languorous nuptials of the Vienne and the Loire, or making your way to Candes-Saint-Martin, where the man who brought the Gospel to France passed away. Legend has it that, as Saint Martin's

Pages 114–15
"The reigns of the Valois scattered their châteaux down the Loire Valley."
D. T.
The spectacular Château de Chenonceau built on the Cher River.

Facing page
Francis I's spiral staircase pierced with wide openings that gives onto the courtyard at the Château de Blois.

corpse was being ferried to Tours, the hawthorn bloomed along the entire course of the river. Just one more legend among so many surrounding this saint of Hungarian stock and onetime mercenary in the Roman legion. It was he who began the Christianization of the country, founding Ligugé, France's first monastery. Saint Martin, as much as Clovis, represents the dawn of our history; hence the emotion standing before the basilica erected to his memory.

I'm not partial to the Château de Saumur. Poor proportions, lumpen symmetry with four octagonal towers. On the other hand, I always enjoy hunting for an Eugénie Grandet through the streets around the church of Saint-Pierre. I'm a bit of a Saumur habitué. There are literature and wine festivals every spring. In the land of Rabelais, this is no contradiction. The gourmet with a goblet in one hand and a quill in the other is a venerable French tradition. One is held in Fontevrault, within the abbey close, by the tomb of Eleanor of Aquitaine. It's much the same the following morning with a countryman's breakfast: crackling *grattons*, black pudding, potted-meat rillettes, Saumur wines, as much as you like. I take my quarters in an ancient abbey turned into an inn at Chênehutte, downstream from Saumur. France is full of abbeys. The good life and monasticism go hand in hand along the whole course of the river. One comes across an island with trees reflected on the water in the rising sun. On the other bank, a bell tower and a village in the mist: it looks like another island. Further on, a row of poplars and another hamlet. Black roofs, white walls, a boat alongside. At sundown the sky waxes yellow and pink: it all looks ineffably gentle. Much the same between Gennes and Saint-Mathurin, where certain old houses on the left bank prove the most elegant in the whole valley. It was on the metal bridge at Gennes that, in 1940, the cadets of Saumur, with a zeal born of desperation, fought heroically against the Germans, simply for the honor of their uniform.

I don't really know the Loire around Nantes. I've seen its flooded meadows mostly from a speeding train. I like, though, to meet it once more where the river throws itself into the ocean—Saint-Nazaire, Le Pouliguen, La Baule, Le Croisic. I remember a dinner at the end of the estuary with two other writers in a "historic" restaurant clinging to the rocks lashed by the waves. Salt-crusted sea bass, a specialty of the house. After seeing Guérande and the Brière once more, it was both agreeable and fitting to watch the Loire die there and chat about books.

Pages 118–19
The *grèves*, banks of straw-colored sand that divide the river bed, inspired this 1923 picture by Félix Vallotton.

Facing page
"At Chaumont... one has to approach the château from the right bank.... Chaumont is the one in which I would most liked to have lived." D. T.

Pages 122–23
"At sundown the sky waxes yellow and pink: it all looks ineffably gentle." D. T.

Merry, beautiful, and honest Touraine,
whose seven valleys stream with water and wine.

Honoré de Balzac

From the Vouvray of Touraine to the Muscadet from the area around Nantes,
the white wines of the Loire Valley are the ideal accompaniment
to an exploration of the region.

Gigantic jewel, as big as
a mountain, cut like a cameo,
and as dainty as lace.
The nearer I approached
the greater my admiration
grew, for nothing in the world
could be more wonderful
or more perfect.

Guy de Maupassant,
La Légende du Mont Saint-Michel

A Family Home

Stately home, homestead, converted barn: the French have a soft spot for a roof and four walls inherited back in the land of their ancestors. Our rustic atavism has left us with a prickly sense of property that manifests itself by our lording over a handful of acres enhanced by its accumulated memories. Its size matters not: provided it is still haunted by the shades of the lineage, a thatched cottage surrounded by a handkerchief-sized sward procures as much emotion as a huge charterhouse standing in landscaped parkland.

My compatriots live mainly in cities or suburbs; often they visit the family house, where a grandmother or an old uncle live, solely during vacations. But it is no less their home port, the place where their history began, and a rallying-point for kith and kin. It is not its denizens that count. They live and then they die. A house though has the gift of eternal youth: restored and occupied, it becomes as spruce as a new bride. If not every Frenchman has the privilege of possessing a family home, almost all more or less secretly desire the roots it provides.

The house might have been in the family for donkey's years, or it may have been purchased by a father or a grandfather keen to be able to lodge his scions under one roof come vacation time. A generation of summer memories is enough to endow the owner with secondhand patriotism for the Franche-Comté, Picardy, or Saintonge. He will do his level best to "attach" the children to the house and get them to return often so they identify with it emotionally. Everybody knows somebody who, to this very end, had a swimming pool dug in an orchard, converted the attic into a games' room, and put up scores of buddies armed with guitars.

The French maintain the instinct to dig a burrow out of their local soil, to make it their headquarters and their castle. If the rich might benefit from a villa in Deauville or a chalet in Chamonix, that will merely be for leisure or for chic, except if they are Norman or Savoyard. The patriotism the French invoke is bound up more with the family residence, and that can be in ruins, falling down, or located out in the sticks where no one wants to go. However that may be, they'll only sell up in direst need. The least well-off inherit no more than a tumbledown cattle shed. They revamp it as their means allow, leaving the wooden beams visible in homage

Page 126
"The Mont Saint-Michel, fabulous floating island." D. T.

Facing page
"The memories they share at the fireside are further cultivated by the photographs of their forebears hanging on the walls." D. T.

to that long-lost age when their clog-wearing forebears tilled the land. Meanwhile, as poor as a church mouse, the last in a noble line shivers, huddled over a wood-burning stove in a wing of a stately home. All the finer pieces of furniture are in rooms he has opened to a paying public so as to be able to repair the roof. The scarcely less down-at-heel heirs to the late-lamented country upper-middle-classes occupy, at least in the summer months, a pile in its historic state without central heating but with damp walls and a leaking roof. The gate squeaks with rust, the enclosing wall has seen better days, and the kitchen garden has run to brambles. But hints of an arbor, some steps up to the grand entrance, the tin dishes on the Henry II dresser, the Christofle silver, and the out-of-tune Gaveau piano attest to a more illustrious past, whose myths the present-day family keeps alive. That complicity with the memory of the nation's rural origins is close to French hearts.

A family home embodies a bond that transcends social class: farmstead or great house, a dwelling is ennobled by the years. Proletarians are just as proud of a parchment document of title attesting to the impressive length of the family's ownership as anyone.

In my village nobody is rich and every family has seen most of its offspring move on to pastures new; it's a question of survival. The Dutch and the English, fond of our lifestyle and scenery, have purchased "second homes" there. Nevertheless, the immense majority of properties in the village remain in the hands of a local family. Admittedly, the shutters often stay shut eleven months out of twelve. But, at the return of summer, the owners of the "estate" throw them open, mow the lawn, and unpack a garden table, a parasol, and deckchairs. Here they are, back home, no less than their ancestors. Some settle for good on their retirement, with the comforting feeling that they have finally looped the loop. They plan a vegetable patch, raise a wall, plant trees, add a lean-to or an awning or two. The memories they share at the fireside are cultivated by the photographs of their forebears on the walls.

For the French, such a house is less "home sweet home" than a Holy Grail or the last vestige of a paradise lost. Hence the air of lofty melancholy it exudes whenever its owners forsake it. A "For Sale" sign seems demeaning. "They shouldn't have," we say to ourselves. Still, everyone knows that the tax department couldn't care less about the continuity of the line and that a family home requires bottomless pockets.

"La Marseillaise"

Just let the first bars resound (*"Allons enfants de la patrie.i.i.e.e"*), and I have a lump in my throat and a shiver running down my spine! Today, like the time I used to go with my father to watch the French soccer team at the Parc des Princes or the rugby at Colombes. When you grow up, I would tell myself, you too, like Raymond Kopa or Adrien Domec, will wear the shirt, and your day of glory will have arrived.

"La Marseillaise" could also be heard on television on the rare occasions General de Gaulle—that is, the boss—appeared on it. This was History with a capital "H." History in majesty ran through my veins without my knowing what any of it actually meant. I too would have liked to be dispatched on a mission by the chief to defy evil and to defend the motherland, like d'Artagnan or a comic strip hero. The national anthem represents my patriotism at its most raw and gutsy. Martial without being militaristic, tragic but not grim, it bounds along as a splendidly arrogant hymn to joy with a verve that (we should admit) manifests something of a low-level, and hence acceptable, superiority complex. The France it exalts has undergone woe and suffering, but it has, in the end, emerged triumphant. Its roll call of battle harks back to Philip II Augustus at Bouvines, Joan of Arc at Orléans, Bayard in Marignan, Condé at Rocroi, the *sans-culottes* at Valmy, the *poilus* in the trenches of Verdun, Alphonse Juin at Monte Cassino. It is France unbuttoned, not on its best behavior: insolent, intrepid, a bit lippy. Proud, even, and ever young at heart.

One day, in my former life, I landed at the airport of an African capital next to then President Jacques Chirac. He descended the airplane steps. Red carpet, worthies with epaulettes, gleaming soldiery, and "La Marseillaise," as was only right, belting out weirdly under the equatorial sun. Hoisting us above our station, at its call we felt invested with a kind of sacramental duty. By extending beyond its borders, the France to which we were paying homage seemed elevated into an ideal. I stood stock-still, saluting. What I felt was quite paradoxical, because in general an official ceremony inspires in me little but an ethnographer's curiosity. I usually have the impression of being a child who has snuck in to watch a play for grown-ups. This time, however, I was sincerely moved.

Facing page
"Every time I hear the French national anthem I feel myself overcome by irrational pride and think myself capable of all manner of daring deeds with an especial paroxysm at the final bar: *Aux armes citoyens!*" D. T. Rouget de Lisle composing "La Marseillaise." Painting by J.-J. Scherrer.

The Sea

As a card-carrying French landlubber, I can never find my sea legs and I swim like a pair of pliers. For me, a week on the open sea is a severe punishment. All in all, I'd prefer a cell in the slammer: at least the floor doesn't bob up and down. I love the sea like crazy, but I keep to the shore, with the promise of a dinner of shellfish washed down with chilled white wine. France is pretty well off in this respect: one ocean and three seas around the mainland, added to two other oceans and one sea in the overseas territories. I have experience of all our ports, beaches, and estuaries and have been bowled over by the lot.

As a child I took the ferry from Calais to Dover and the salty breeze blew on the cliffs. Later, I paddled on the beach at Wissant where de Gaulle used to go on vacation and come nightfall I wandered over the wet cobblestones in Boulogne's upper town. I must even have lost a coin or two at the casino, down by the waterfront. And other memories at Montreuil, which the sea has since forsook, of Dieppe, Varengeville (Georges Braque's tomb stands beside the church), Fécamp, Yport, on the track of Georges Simenon. From the roads off Bénouville, the cliffs look mysterious. One can see the menhir carved by the spume that Gustave Courbet immortalized and against which perhaps his famous *Wave* once crashed. Suddenly Étretat emerges, enclosed in its tiny valley: a harmony of gray roofs that turn pink as glittering sun passes under the Aiguille Creuse. Even without Monet, Boudin, Courbet, and Maupassant, even without Arsène Lupin (the gentleman thief who concludes one of his adventures in the *Aiguille Creuse*), it would still be magical. Behind the "Hollow Needle," one can see, as one skirts the golf course, the cliffs cut out against another.

We are on the borderlands of a Pays de Caux of austere flatness. Multicolored houses of brick and pinkish flint add to the charm. The granddaughter of Arsène Lupin's creator Maurice Leblanc purchased the estate in which he wrote quite a few of his books, but ended her days in lunacy. A passably eccentric house, too, adorned with a covered patio and a bower.

Le Havre: the view of the refinery port and the estuary from the hill at Sainte-Adresse. Nothing could be more reinvigorating than the cliff-top road through luxuriant greenery between

Facing page
The sea approached from the shore. At the end of this shady path, the water of the Emerald Coast in northern Brittany.

Pages 136–37
"Suddenly, Étretat emerges, enclosed in its tiny valley: a harmony of gray roofs that turn pink as the glittering sun passes under the Aiguille Creuse." D. T.

Honfleur and Trouville where I like to hunt for childhood memories along the boardwalk as far as the Roches Noires. I built sand castles opposite the Trouville Palace Hotel. Later in life, I ate my fill of mussels and baby sole at Les Vapeurs. Cabourg is Proust's Balbec, but I prefer the town of Houlgate. Fog at Ouistreham, the fishermen in Port-en-Bessin who set sail at midnight in January when the scallop season comes. I stayed there once, finishing a book. At night I could see the lights of the boats from my perch at the Marines, close to the pier. White tombstones in the American cemetery at Omaha Beach, meadows where cows graze suspended above the cliffs. There are always cliffs. The Mont Saint-Michel, that fabulous floating island, the Cotentin at Saint-Vaast, in Tocqueville, in Cherbourg, in Carteret with a thought for Barbey d'Aurevilly. I recall the boat at Granville that would ferry me to the island of Chausey.

Then darker-hued rocks: Brittany. Perros-Guirec, Paimpol, Saint-Malo, the Brest roadstead on a sloop (at anchor), Audierne Bay, Concarneau. More memories still and some of love since girls like being chatted up at the seaside, it softens their heart. The bourgeois charm of La Baule, the less bourgeois charm of Les Sables-d'Olonne, the all too often concreted-over beaches of the Vendée. Two towers, the old port, the magic of La Rochelle, with another memory of a love affair. I can just see myself with a girl, really young, as blond as could be, beneath the arcades of Simenon's "phantom of the hatter." The writer had lived nearby, describing its white light and capturing that odd impression near Esnandes and Marcilly, where the mussel beds make it hard to know where dry land ends and the sea begins. A similar impression at the edge of the Gironde estuary, where the endless beach of the Landes starts, to stop only at the Basin of Arcachon. Another ambivalent place, with other memories: the timeworn charm of the city in winter, one evening during an almighty storm at Hortense's. Another love story! The seashore is conducive. As a student in Bordeaux I used to go flirting in Contis, on a dune between two oceans, the midnight blue Atlantic and the dark green pines. I have crossed this beach of the Landes on foot, between Mimizan and Boucau, with Jean-Paul Kauffmann and our sons. Bracing, perhaps, but caked in crude oil.

From Bayonne to Ciboure, the oval ball hovers above the ocean, and I am on more familiar territory. Behind the facade of a seaside resort of no particular interest, except for surfers, Hossegor delights in a casino in a fairly remarkable Basque-cum-Béarn art deco style.

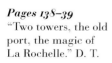

Pages 138–39
"Two towers, the old
port, the magic of
La Rochelle." D. T.

Right
Blackish rocks: Brittany
buffeted by late fall
gales in the Finistère.

I wrote the script for a TV film at Arcangues dreaming of the writer Paul-Jean Toulet. I have reveled in more virile and sporty emotions at Piquesarry, Saint-Léon, Aguilera. Biarritz, a sanctuary for my nostalgia. I return there each winter, during the week. It rains on the neo-Gothic follies, on the Palace, and on the Bellevue casino—two outcrops of a cardboard-cutout anglomania—and it rains on the beach between the two rocks, on the Royalty restaurant, and on the pretty station where trains no longer deign to halt. Biarritz is a very venerable lady, who, in some indefinite past, wreaked stormy havoc on the Rocher de la Vierge. She can still smile about it as she wheels her golf-cart over the driveways of the Chiberta course, while the boats sail out of the Adour.

Another rugby-enchanted shoreline: the Roussillon. At the foot of the vineyards, between Port-Vendres and Collioure, this was Matisse's kingdom. Cézanne hunkered down among the white rocks around Marseille, and, high above the Joliette, verses wander into my memory. Or a speech from Marcel Pagnol, interpreted by the actor Raimu. Toulon is no looker, but the roadstead is majestic and the old quarter around the rue d'Alger or the cours Lafayette has real soul. I love our Mediterranean, as much as our Atlantic; it is the original Mare Nostrum, our share of Hellenism and Romanitas, our invitation to Africa, the most familiar mirage in our quest for joy. Are the landscapes it etches out more beautiful on Corsica than on the Riviera? Who knows. My memories of the Gulf of Saint-Florent, of the bars of Bastia, of a flowery creek in Solenzara, of Calvi, where the white kepis of the legionnaires stand out against an ocher citadel, are in any case wonderful. The nationalists who make the front page may be short on charm, but all the Corsicans I have met have been delightful; their introverted nature makes me think of the Auvergnats. They have that reserve common to mountain people, the same rough-and-ready pride round the edges, and the same reaction if they feel got at: they snap shut like oysters.

Right
"I love our Mediterranean . . . it is the original Mare Nostrum, our share of Hellenism and Romanitas . . . the most familiar mirage in our quest for joy." D. T.
The *calanques* of Cassis, a realm of creeks much loved by Cézanne, Matisse, Dufy, and Signac, to name but a few.

Still damp, the Bay of Somme gloomily reflects
an Egyptian sky, raspberry, turquoise, and ashen green.
Has the sea perhaps retreated so far that it will never return?
But it will return, treacherous and furtive as I know she is here.

Colette

Beach huts dotted along the beach
at the Bay of Somme.

Tintin's Marlinspike Hall

By modeling Marlinspike Hall (Moulinsart in the original) approximately on the château of Cheverny, Tintin's creator, the Walloon Hergé, was actually imagining the ideal venue for the perfect French retirement: a reasonably sized country house in an extensive park. Marlinspike Hall is a haven of calm and delight where, between two adventures, Tintin joins Captain Haddock for bucolic wanderings in the garden. Tintin himself has no roots. Haddock stumbled across his family ancestry, the property having belonged to one of his forefathers, a corsair by trade (in *Red Rackham's Treasure*). Marlinspike Hall remains a provisional—not to say illusory—haven, as Tintin is always dragging the old seadog away from it. But the place materializing these hopes for escape is a real domain, and Cheverny well and truly exists: a million tourists crossing the Loire Valley have seen it with their own eyes. The parallel springs to mind immediately when one glimpses its two domed ranges reposing on a carpet of greenery like a splendid jewel. It has to be Marlinspike Hall. It is easy to imagine it peopled by Professor Calculus, the soprano Castafiore, Jolyon Wagg, Abdullah, and various prowlers. One feels one could go looking for "Cutts the Butcher's" near the church of Cour-Cheverny. A Tintin museum has sprung up in a former outhouse: it features Calculus's shark-shaped submarine, laboratory, and pendulum. One meets Nestor in his butler's uniform: it's as if he might take your coat at the bottom of the main staircase or offer a glass of the master's best malt. For the magic to work on our imagination, Cheverny just had to be a Loire château, located in a real village in the provinces: noble enough but not princely, of "classical" appearance, snug behind its walls, with venerable trees and manicured lawns as far as the eye can see. The owners' lineage is of course patrician, without being particularly eminent. It is a delight to venture down the avenues of the park as the sun sets, preferably after a day of a cloudless blue. One feels at home, or almost, just like Tintin striding about Marlinspike Hall with its owner complete with riding breeches, a riding crop, and monocle. Any blue-blooded Frenchman would love to retire to "Moulinsart," with or without a Nestor. All it requires is to unearth an adventurous forebear enterprising enough to have brought back a treasure.

Facing page
"Cheverny (a.k.a 'Marlinspike Hall') is historical but still homely. Its charm is overwhelming but never intimidating. Superbly graceful and sober in its lines, the greenery in which the whole building nestles is wonderfully gentle." D.T.
In *The Seven Crystal Balls* Tintin and Snowy arrive in Marlinspike Hall, which Hergé modeled on Cheverny.

Nous y sommes...

Bonjour, Nestor. Le capi-
taine est-il là ?

Non, monsieur Tintin,
monsieur est sorti : il est
allé faire une promenade
à cheval...

Mais il ne tardera
pas à rentrer.
Voyez...

Voilà déjà son cheval...

Et voilà monsieur...

Bonjour, capitaine !...

Bonjour, mon ami,
bonjour... Un instant,
vous per-mettez ?...

Nestor !... Nestor !...
Un autre, je vous prie...

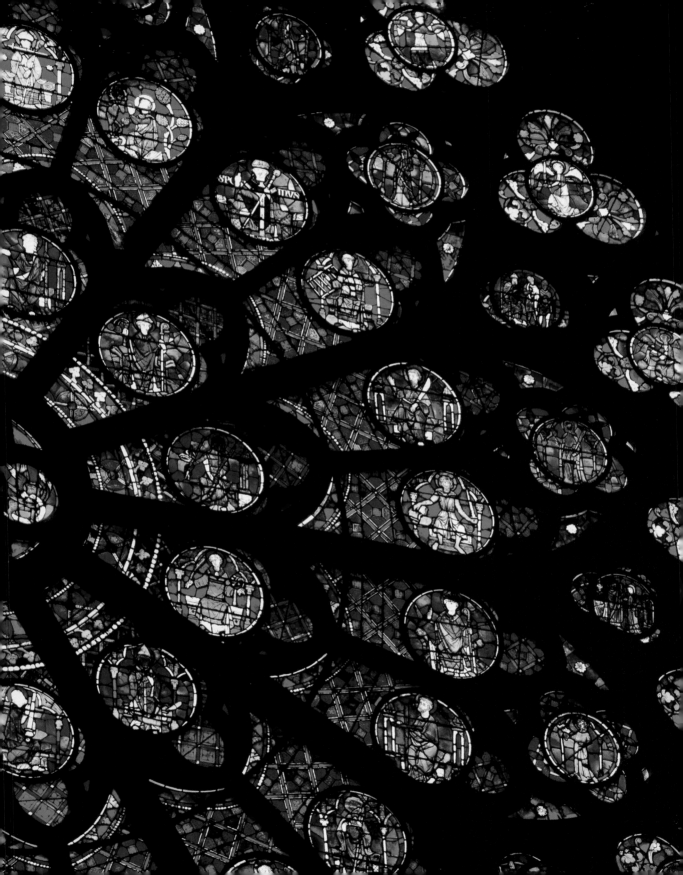

See Notre-Dame over there. Creation, the history of the world, dogmas, virtues, the lives of saints, arts and crafts, everything we knew then was taught by its porch and its stained glass windows.

Paul Cézanne

Notre-Dame Cathedral

I, who am neither king nor prince, like to view it from every side. As I amble through it, I can feel it vibrate with—how can I put it?—well, the soul of France. Or its heart. Or whatever in it will last forever. Gazing out from the Pont de Sully on the arches of the apse fanning out like a wheat sheaf, pleasure dissolves into gravity and pride. Further joy on catching sight of the rose window at the end of the rue Maître-Albert, and another running the eyes along the statues on the tympanum. Each time, I spot a face or a gesture I hadn't noticed before. And each time, walking round it, as I inspect the fabulous tangle of arches, capitals, turrets, and gargoyles, it is as if I can see the hulking shadow of its hunchback, Quasimodo, with Esmeralda under his arm. Because my vision of Notre-Dame and its quarter derives entirely from Victor Hugo's novel—a romantic drama inspired by its Gothic splendor, a literary cathedral, one of many, and inimitably French, with a monster with a heart of gold and a pure gypsy. Oddly, mass tourism, unbearable everywhere else, here neither irritates nor offends me; the Japanese, the Americans gazing open-mouthed on the rood screen are in a way simply the successors of the long line of believers who, since Saint Louis, have made their way here to pray and to admire. Even if the twofold mystery of the humanity and resurrection of Christ (the subject of the carvings) arouses in them no more than polite curiosity. Just let the organ burst out during High Mass on Sunday and, I fondly hope, they must surely feel that France weighs more than its GDP.

Other French cathedrals of this triumphant Gothic emerged at the same time: Laon, Beauvais, Noyon, Senlis, Amiens (that Ruskin thought the finest), Orléans, Bourges, Chartres, Rouen, Reims. Some are more elegant and each harbors at least a fragment of our national genius, a piece of its memory. But Notre-Dame, located on the most ancient island of the Cité; Notre-Dame, around which *clerkes* studying under Albertus Magnus, Saint Thomas Aquinas, and Sorbon, gamboled; Notre-Dame, at the edge of the river where ghosts of our poets flit between the secondhand booksellers and the taverns; Notre-Dame de Paris, of which Édith Piaf sings so tenderly, at once concentrates and elevates the diverse spirituality that rings out from the bell towers of this antique land.

Page 148
The south rose window in Notre-Dame de Paris.

Facing page
"Gazing out from the Pont de Sully on the arches of the apse fanning out like a wheat sheaf, pleasure dissolves into gravity and pride."
D. T.

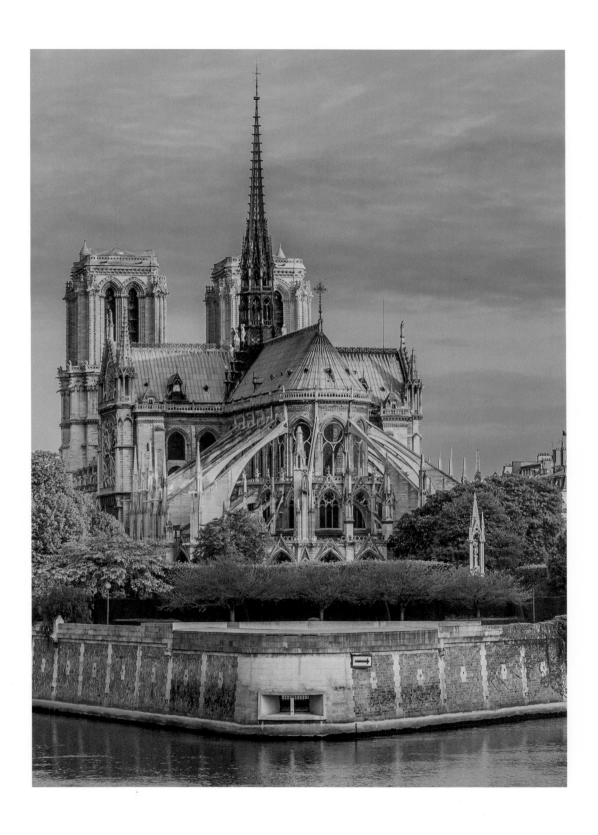

A walk about Paris
will provide lessons
in history, beauty,
and in the point of life.

Thomas Jefferson

Baguette

We have entered a new era for the bakery and this ancient tradition is recruiting misty-eyed adepts to the craft. Ovens are being restored here and there and those who love making their own bread are even building new ones. But this is more than just a pleasure. There is pride in harking back to a venerable cult; and a feeling of self-sufficiency too, perhaps. If there's a war, or a revolution, or famine, at least they'll have bread. Because bread remains *the* symbol of human food. At least for the French. Good bread, white or brown, wheat or rye: only France really knows how to knead and bake it.

Baguette, *ficelle, couronne*: I like to see and breathe them in at the bakery counter. No one knows why but bakers are almost always in a good mood. I like to stroke the dusting of flour of a nice big farmhouse loaf. And more than anything I like to bite my teeth into the heel of a baguette. It is the baguette that best illustrates the supremacy of French bread and, as if by chance, caricaturists put it under every Frenchman's arm, to go with the beret on his head. Van Gogh got its color—straw yellow, gilded, and orangey—just right and captured its peaks and troughs to a T. Perhaps he was also inspired by its slender form. For me, it is the tastiest, the most carnal of breads. It should be eaten at the bar, split lengthwise and buttered, with a *café crème* in the morning, a ritual repeated at lunchtime with a "Paris-beurre." Paris, queen of the baguette, though provincial bakers need have no inferiority complex. The whole world envies us. Why then do chic restaurants persist in laying on fussy rolls laden with nuts, grapes, bacon pieces, and sesame seeds? Wherefore the newfangled multigrain? Nothing accompanies a meal better than a hunk of wheat baguette. Not a tin loaf. Not a "brioche." A real Paris baguette, as honest as the day is long.

Page 152
The polychrome marble grand staircase at the Opéra, Paris. Its architect, Charles Garnier, designed it as a temple to the arts of luxury and pleasure.

Facing page
"It is the baguette that best illustrates the supremacy of French bread and, as if by chance, caricaturists put it under every Frenchman's arm, to go with the beret on his head." D. T. Baguette and beret here snapped by the famous American photographer Elliott Erwitt.

Paris, Queen of the World

"Paris, reine du monde" (queen of the world) goes the song. A queen, undoubtedly, but of an often icy arrogance. Like Queen Margot, who used to take lovers when the fancy took her only to cast them off so they would die of despair. Yet she can be an incomparable lover if she sees fit. "Paris is a blond," the same ditty continues. Blond, or nearly blond in the sunshine, languishing voluptuously on the banks of the Seine, but gray in a downpour when the chill of Haussmann's style prevails, if softened by the patterns of her wrought-iron balconies, never one the same, that seem to throw strips of black lace over the facades.

With Rome, it is the most beautiful capital in the world. For an artist, a diplomat, an "honest man"; it was also, between Louis XIV and World War II, the center of the civilized world. A haven for outlaws, a shimmering mirage for lovers on the run, a dangerous trap for provincials. It has been fantasized about, lusted after. Some thought they had it in the palm of their hand, others wasted a fortune in it, receiving in exchange nothing more than a wan smile. Yet one flees it without ceasing to love it, body and soul. Sooner or later one returns to hide out in the Latin Quarter. The only "Latin" thing, it must be said, in this city of the north: something one notices the minute one ventures out of one of its six rail stations. What coldness! It so ruined my childhood that I'm still a bit mistrustful. What can this gorgeous seductress hold in store for me? Even disregarding her necklace of jewels glinting along the riverside, her architectural treasures, her two enchanted islands, her two sacred hillocks and her churches, all of which I know through and through, there remain her strewn fragments of the most wonderful urban jigsaw in the world. Out of ordinary memories and wanderings we all reconstruct our own Paris. I have a weakness for the place Saint-Georges, the Mouzaïa, Batignolles, Père-Lachaise, the Grand Boulevards between the République and the porte Saint Martin, the public garden in the shape of a ship's stern at the end of the Île Saint-Louis, the Passy of the place de Costa-Rica, the church and the sloping cemetery of Charonne, the Porte Dorée with the art deco frontage of the now defunct Musée des Colonies. I felt the same in Belleville and Ménilmontant, in the Halles before they were relocated, the area around the

Facing page
"Paris, the most wonderful urban jigsaw puzzle in the world."
D. T.
The living visual symbol of Paris and France, the Eiffel Tower inspired painters, such as Seurat in 1889.

Bastille, the Canal Saint-Martin. But these have changed so much that I no longer feel at home there, so I tend to retrench to the fundamentals: a circle circumscribed by the Luxembourg, the Montagne Sainte-Geneviève, the place Maubert, the rue du Bac, and the Seine. Around Odéon, there flit so many phantoms dear to writers that, despite the proliferation of banks, fast-food chains, and T-shirt boutiques, I feel protected against the slings and arrows of the present century. In short, there I have the impression of living at the center of the civilized world. More intelligence is wasted here than consumed on all five continents. To no purpose, alas, because the Paris intelligentsia has a penchant for nihilism, and, in the long run, the glumness wears you down. I end up going round and round in circles within this gilded castle in the air. At that point, I make my escape.

Praise be, beguiling Paris conceals an abundance of mysteries, both captivating and poisonous. I climb out of my hole, zigzag haphazardly, and each time I'm sure to be rewarded with some unexpected vista from the bar of some unknown bistro, and here I am, head over heels in love again with Paris, queen of the world.

Montmartre is one of two sacred mountains in Paris. For a long time I was reluctant to ever venture there, due to the church of the Sacré-Cœur, so ugly, so absurdly "oriental," so bourgeois and over-the-top, so dreadfully fin de siècle. And then there are the hordes of tourists on place du Tertre. I kept to its fringes, on the southern slope, where the bargirls hang out, on rues Fontaine, Ballu, de Douai, Pigalle; a gently rising buffer zone that leads up to Montmartre proper from the Nouvelle Athènes and the Quartier de l'Europe, via place Blanche and place Pigalle. Forty years ago it was like being in a Bohemian novel. The neon signs in these bars attracted me like a moth, but the glass of champagne excited my libido without quenching it. Hardly perched on the barstool that I had to slink off: I never had the money for more than one. Then, together with a drinking companion, I'd dive across the boulevard de Clichy, clamber up rue Lepic, and we'd wend our way to rue Berthe or Ravignan, up to place Jean-Baptiste Clément.

No hipsters there yet! No more street urchins either. Just cats. Later I haunted the northern slopes, obsessed by rue Caulaincourt, which I find so romantic where it gives out onto place Constantin Pecqueur. Meanwhile, I had learned about the people living on the hillock between the construction of a Gallo-Roman temple and the

Facing page
"Grace, unaffectedness, an elegance imprinted with as much sobriety as majesty. An equilibrium characteristic of everything built in France between the reigns of Louis XII and Louis XVI. The Invalides: perfection in volume, modesty in decorum." D. T.

painters' retreat to Montparnasse after World War I. The abbey, the oath of Ignatius Loyola with his six companions, Henry IV's *Te Deum* after his abjuration ("Paris is well worth a Mass"), the Cossack incursion (1814), then the English (1815), the Commune (inspiring Jean-Baptiste Clément's song "Le Temps des Cerises"), the election of Clemenceau as mayor. And I filled the Butte with the writers (Flaubert, Gautier, Nerval, Baudelaire, etc.) and painters (Delacroix, Corot, almost all the impressionists, etc.) who compose its legend. From the cabaret of the Chat Noir (Bruant) to the Moulin-Rouge (Toulouse-Lautrec), via the Lapin Agile and the Moulin de la Galette, my imagination rebuilds all the long-vanished windmills veering between the death throes of romanticism and the demise of the Belle Époque. While I have met the occasional Mimi Pinson (Musset), I never met an epigone of the painter Suzanne Valadon. The age was no longer particularly literary. Now it is less so than ever, and yet the magic of Montmartre remains undimmed, or almost. Nowadays I always approach the Butte along rue Caulaincourt and mount avenue Junot, avoiding rue Norvins and losing myself up the slope to which clings the sorry vineyard and the cemetery of Saint-Vincent. Novelist Marcel Aymé and painter Gen Paul are both buried there. Rue des Saules, rue Cortot, rue du Mont-Cenis, rue du Chevalier-de-la-Barre. I am fatally drawn to that side, whence one can see the greenish roof of the Basilica of Saint-Denis and, on match nights, the floodlights of the Stade de France. I fly as fast as possible across place du Tertre to look down on the panorama. Paris lies all around, wrapped in fog. I am moved by the roofline, all gray-black zinc, all different, graced with a myriad of little orange chimneys in the shape of top hats around which pigeons scratch. No dormer window, no fanlight resembles another; the whole looks like a song by Piaf. Plainly, the "Môme" has said all there is to say about the soul of Paris.

Montmartre, a holy hill, but a toxic one if you dare to walk up it on rainy weekdays late at night, when you become a voyeur trying to fathom an incomprehensible mystery. Place Clichy remains a welcome border crossing whence you can slip down rue Cavalotti and take refuge in the Bouclard restaurant where everything is good. I use it as my canteen every so often and I pour my friends a decent Côte de Nuits. To walk off the drink, we walk across the cemetery bisected by rue Caulaincourt, before pushing on to rue de Clignancourt, another border, and landing in a local bar. Fewer and fewer tourists. One can also climb up rue Lamarck, lined with

pleasant enough restaurants. After midnight, everyone is either off to bed or has retrenched in the wine bars on rue des Abbesses. No more tourists. The Butte now belongs to the cats and to the shades of poets, traveling acrobats, and lovers. This is my time of day. I walk up and down the staircases, prowling about searching for that mysterious something, or nothing, that I covet only here.

Montagne Sainte-Geneviève. Jean de Meung wrote the second version of the *Romance of the Rose* in rue Saint-Jacques, while Verlaine expired in rue Descartes, so the hill where Lutetia morphed into Paris witnessed both the dawn and the twilight of French poetry. After World War II, on the place de la Contrescarpe, a student at Polytechnique could walk past his counterpart from the École Normale on the rue d'Ulm, or a modern troubadour, thereby sustaining a double tradition to which the library, the Lycées of Henri-IV and Louis-le-Grand, and the taverns on the Montagne Sainte-Geneviève still attest.

This is the slope by the Sorbonne that rises toward Saint-Nicolas-du-Chardonnet (classicism). The other flank played host to craft shops (rue Mouffetard) and the great unwashed (Faubourg Saint-Jacques). At the bottom of "La Mouffe," after the market, stands Saint-Médard (late Gothic). On the fringes of the faubourg, Saint-Jacques-du-Haut-Pas (Jansenist austerity), then the chapel of the Val-de-Grâce (baroque *à la française*). These are then the frontier posts of a *montagne* to which I feel myself drawn instinctively whenever the lower town gets on my nerves. Just after World War I, Hemingway spent part of his youth at the top of rue du Cardinal-Lemoine, the inspiration for *A Moveable Feast*, a pagan hymn to the spirits of this sacred place where Guise's Liguards—if Dumas in *La Dame de Montsoreau* is to be credited—plotted the assassination of Henry III in the former Dominican convent. "Sacred" it might be but, holy cow, generations of *escholiers* here have downed tankard after tankard of wine or hydromel, and chased the innkeeper's daughter.

In gratitude to God for preserving Louis XV, Soufflot erected a clunky church since converted into an ideological temple: the Panthéon. Though the style strives to be in the same vein, its dome is bereft of the elegance of the Invalides, the Institut de France, the Val-de-Grâce, the chapel at the Sorbonne, and Saint-Paul. It seems a secret went missing between the two Louis, XIII and XV. The Panthéon is foursquare and chilly, macabre and prissy:

Facing page
"Out of ordinary memories and wanderings we all reconstruct our own Paris.... I have a weakness for the Canal Saint-Martin. But it has changed so much that I no longer feel at home there." D. T.

Pages 166–67
"The grace of Saint-Étienne-du-Mont is natural, with a certain aesthetic carelessness in the contrast between the tower, the front, the nave, and the rood screen." D. T.

it lacks soul. In any case not the light, reflective, spring-like, and burgeoning soul of Saint-Étienne-du-Mont, where a Renaissance stem is interwoven with a sprig of baroque. The manes of Clotilde and Clovis rule over this charming disorder as over a conquered land. Here, next to her tombstone, shimmers a shrine containing the relics of Sainte Geneviève. And there, beneath the piers of the chapel to the rear, repose the remains of Racine and Pascal. Each time I enter this church, I am beset by an emotion that has nothing to do with nostalgia. Each time I emerge from it, I do so having reached a joyful and flattering conclusion: untrammeled, the French genius is simply incomparable. The grace of Saint-Étienne-du-Mont is natural, with a certain aesthetic carelessness in the contrast between the tower, the front, the nave, and the rood screen. Misgivings were unknown under the last Valois and the first Bourbons: the new was built over the old, as inspiration struck and by the grace of God.

In the chapel of the Saint-Sépulcre, an anonymous seventeenth-century picture shows Christ crucified above the Virgin, Saint John, Saint Louis, King Louis XIII, and Aristotle in a line. The presence of Louis XIII is merely Caesar's due; the king must have paid hand over fist, and unwillingly, since he was a skinflint. But I am surprised and charmed by how the painter includes the greatest of the philosophers. A plaque hangs to remind us out what the Montagne owes the Jacobins, those disciples of Saint Dominic: Albertus Magnus and Saint Thomas Aquinas taught round the corner, ensuring Aristotle a place on the syllabus.

The soaring cost of real estate means the district has become gentrified. The École Polytechnique has emigrated to the suburbs, the cabarets on the Contrescarpe—where songsters Georges Brassens, Jacques Brel, Barbara, Jean Ferrat, Claude Nougaro, Félix Leclerc, Jacques Bertin, and consorts all began—have closed down, and aspiring *normaliens* are less well-read than their elders. Less wacky too. With all its Greek restaurants "La Mouffe" feels like the outskirts of Piraeus. One may still discern, however, on this mountainside sprouting with narrow lanes, the presence of the down-at-heel intelligentsia instead of trendy hipsterdom, and the parishioners leaving Saint-Étienne-du-Mont may seem to have read Villon or Verlaine instead of a social commentator gone viral.

If you are lucky enough to have lived in Paris
as a young man, then wherever you go for the rest of your life,
it stays with you, for Paris is a moveable feast.

Ernest Hemingway

"Hemingway spent part of his youth at the top of rue du Cardinal-Lemoine,
the inspiration for *A Moveable Feast.*" D. T.
Place de la Concorde, in front of the Fontaine des Fleuves.

Basque Country

Before getting to know the Basque Country, I had dreamed about it and longed for it after reading *Ramuntcho*, by Pierre Loti. A village nestling in a little valley, hamlets scattered on the slopes of the Pyrenees. Whitewashed houses, thickset churches, ocher *frontons* with a curved pediment for the game of pelota, men hewn from the rock with a beret on their head and espadrilles on their feet, who speak a language known to no one else.

The clouded Rhune, the Nivelle between Saint-Jean-de-Luz and Ciboure, the Bidasoa river on the French or Spanish side. In the distance, the rattle of the Paris-Irun train. The Bay of Biscay opening out to the Americas to which many adventurous Basques sailed in search of riches. It is a French land, but it is not French like the others. A parenthesis of undulating greenery strewn with white villages trimmed in red half-timbering.

One stumbles upon it suddenly, by way of Bayonne across the bridge over the Adour, or on crossing the same river upstream, at Urt, for example. The pines of the Landes, the maize fields between the floodplains of the "barthes," and the declivities of Chalosse on the level of Peyrehorade are long behind us. On the other bank, once at Bidache, the sense of being somewhere else is dizzying. It is palpable again beneath the arcades at La Bastide-Clairence. One continues one's wanderings down to Saint-Palais and Baïgori, passing by Cambo (where the author of *Cyrano de Bergerac*, Edmond Rostand, owned a villa), by Hasparren where poet Francis Jammes lived in the 1920s and 1930s, by Ainhoa, and by Espelette of pepper fame. The village of Ramuntcho appears as a blend of Sare and Ascain amidst the hills of Urrugne.

This is the Labour, a coastal province of the French Basque Country. Although tourism, as everywhere else, has theme-parked its customs and massacred its coast, French Basque Country remains unfamiliar, magical, ritual, the hinterland especially. Exotic would be going a bit far, though I understand the obduracy of an indigenous population determined to preserve its native language and the animosity of people from Bayonne for those of Pau. Political self-government would be nonsensical and one can hardly approve of the militant *omerta* with respect to terrorists from Spain. Still, in a land that is anything except ordinary, one

Basque Country

Facing page
"French Basque Country remains unfamiliar... the hinterland especially." D. T. Here Ainhoa, very close to the Spanish border.

Pages 172–73
"Men hewn from the rock with a beret on their head.... *Pelotaris* playing with a leather or wicker *xistera* tied to their arm." D. T. Three *xistera* players in a painting in the Basque museum in Bayonne.

can understand the struggle for identity. So much has changed since the Belle Époque when Loti—always one for dollops of local color—wrote his purple passages about the Basque soul rooted in a cult of the past and its unyielding Catholicism. The traitor Ganelon no longer lurks at Roncevaux, where the only perils pilgrims risk on their way to Santiago de Compostela are sunstroke and corns on their feet. There are no more carabineros lying in ambush on the banks of the Nivelle or on the hill paths through the Rhune massif. One is free to buy cigarettes and chorizo at the pass at Ibarzine. Smugglers now use other routes and simply drive over the border. The beret too is vanishing and Basque orthodoxy is on the wane, though on Sunday the church at Sare resounds with canticles sung in Basque and religious processions remain a common sight. Many residents are of "foreign" stock, in particular at the seaside. One needs to be patient to sniff out the charm of Bidart and Guétary among the rows of insipid new bungalows.

All the same, when the Paris-Irun drops you off at Bayonne, Biarritz-La Négresse, or Saint-Jean-de-Luz, you are promptly transported to quite another France. Beneath its ramparts and the spires of its cathedral, Bayonne is the epicenter of Basque uniqueness. Particularly between the Nive and the Adour, where the locals look you up and down with circumspection. Come winter, beneath the rain, when from the Bellevue or the Palais, a hotel as whipped cream as may be imagined, one watches boats making headway out of the Adour, Biarritz is Basque in English dress. Saint-Jean-de-Luz, with its church where Louis XIV dallied with the Spanish Infanta, aristocratically Basque. Crossing the Nivelle, the charms of Ciboure are less exuberant, more rustic, and herald the delights of the mountain villages. A wide berth must be given to the seashore. To witness dancing clouds that paint the mountains soft and luxuriant or dark and menacing, one has instead to progress through its valleys or leap over its brooks. The walls remain spotlessly white, with balconies, studwork, and pitched roofs like a beret on an angular visage. Then, never far from the church, on a space dedicated to the fronton, *pelotaris* playing with a leather or wicker *xistera* tied to their arm. Are they Basques or tourists? No matter. The sport is as it always has been and the posters stuck on the walls announce a *force basque*—a Basque strongman competition. Or a rugby match, another liturgy in this cult of strength, if unknown at the time when the charms of a Basque girl from Gipuzkoa turned Loti's head.

Édith Piaf

Dressed in her perennial black, a trembling, poignant widow of Love. She almost always speaks of love in her songs: that love of loves that paints life *en rose*, the straightforward, miraculous, ideal but physical love of a shopgirl or a prostitute. No executives, no white collars among her open-hearted choices: her lover is an accordionist who can squeeze a waltz, or a legionnaire who smells of burning sand. Guys from Paris, from the wrong side of the tracks, from Belleville (whence she hailed), or Montmartre.

Her heartbreaking voice—like a French Billie Holiday—revives images of my Parisian childhood. The tramp on the Pont de Sully with his pushchair, that poor woman boarding in a maid's room on the sixth floor (no elevator), the chestnut seller on the place Félix-Éboué, traveling acrobats at the Bastille, the Bouglione circus clown. Ah! the somber sadness of the song "Bravo pour le Clown"! The gray gloom of courtyards, of cobbled lanes. Gray rain on gray roofs. The Paris of "Môme Piaf" is one with that of Villon's fourteenth-century verse, Carco's novels, Robert Doisneau's photographs. A unique theater staging its own dramas: Paris "rolled up like a snail round the bells on a church square." (Obviously the one in front of Notre-Dame.) A hopeless tenderness against a backdrop of misery, exalted into poetry by a mocking heart.

Piaf's life was a grim novel, very *noir*; "blacker than the black of my heart" after the death of her lover Cerdan, a boxer on his way to heaven, not a high-hat on the razzle in a cathouse. The street kid, the "Môme Piaf," deals in raw pathos. Her voice is like one long sob, stifled for the sake of decency. Thanks to this voice straight out of a speakeasy the heart of working-class Paris receives its letters of nobility and attains universality. "Beneath the Paris sky birds from the world over come to chatter among themselves." And, on all five continents, I have heard people (though never intellectuals) sing "L'Hymne à l'Amour" or "La Valse de l'Amour." Always love, an immense dream perpetually cheated by those "'I love yous' of July 14, those 'forevers' sold on the cheap." Hence that distraught morality, disguised beneath a roguish irony. And then this sublime anti-morality, the same deep down as Saint Augustine's, a cry from the heart, the soul's confession: "If you love me, I couldn't care a damn about the rest of the world."

Facing page
"Piaf, her heartbreaking voice revives images of my Parisian childhood." D. T.
Photograph taken at the Olympia in 1961.

Provence

Centered on a windmill inhabited by an owl, in *Lettres de mon Moulin* (*Letters from My Windmill*) Alphonse Daudet concocted a fantastical Provence since read by countless schoolchildren. It has illuminated their imagination and that of their parents since the Second French Empire. Before ever going there, I had long dreamed of the flowery, scented land of the *Letters from My Windmill*, in which even an object has a soul, and one in harmony with the innocence and seriousness of a child. I had already visited it with Daudet. I opened a door: white-rumped rabbits bolted, the old owl upstairs remained stock-still. Thus, it was through reading passages like this that I acquired a kind of poetic identity: "It is from this spot that I write to you, with my door wide open, in the warming sun. A pretty wood of pines shining in the light tumbles down to the bottom of the knoll before me. On the horizon, the slender ridge of the Alpilles. Not a sound. Scarcely, from afar, the sound of a pipe, a curlew among the lavender, mules tinkling along the track. And all this gorgeous Provence scenery lives only by dint of the light. So now, why would you think I might miss your noisy, grubby Paris?"

Coincidentally, in Paris I was screwed to the school bench when I would have liked to be cutting out. The cobblestones, walls, roofs, sky, were all of a cold, ashen gray and the odd Sunday detention exacerbated the feeling of being imprisoned. How was I not to cast an envious eye on this land of plenty, of untamed nature, where popes mounted on mules blithely quaff Châteauneuf-du-Pape and where sub-prefects neglect their official duties to pen verses in the shade of the hackberries? Did it all actually exist? I so wanted to believe in it, to be able to grab a map and stick a pin in the destination of my imaginary bid for escape.

As a teenager I hitchhiked there and was bowled over. The concert of the cicadas made my head spin, the colors made my eyes pop—the green of the pastures, the white of the gravel, the misty mauve of the mountainsides, the black of the cypresses. The farmhouses, the herds, the villages inspired in me the same tenderness that Daudet bestows on his characters and their land. It is a tenderness that rhymes with sadness in the stories about the flighty Arlésienne and the knife-grinder: happiness may be there—one just has to lift one's head—but tragedy too is never far away. Thanks be to heaven, there is also comedy, at the very gates of hell, as shown by the bizarre testimony from the hereafter by the "Cucugnan priest" and by the hangovers occasioned by the elixir of Brother Gaucher, exonerated by the orisons of his fellow churchmen. Naive in its country way, a Catholicism of crèches and altar boys orchestrates the passing seasons with its processions and penitents. A theologian would find it wanting for orthodoxy, but I discovered the exoticism I craved.

I have returned there many times to traipse around the windmill. I can hereby attest: Daudet's Provence does indeed exist. It lies within a perimeter circumscribed approximately by the Camargue, the Crau, the Alpilles, and the Rhône. I have dreamt it with my eyes wide open and I have always adored this heavenly realm of absolute Frenchness. Paradise lost: like many writers of the second half of the nineteenth century, Daudet, exiled in Paris, idealized his homeland. But his bucolic, pastoral imagery goes one better than everyday nostalgia since his realism is enhanced with the marvelous. It all stems from his manner of storytelling, like a grandpa talking to a child or an old hand telling a tenderfoot from the city, with a familiarity that pulls the reader in.

Jean Giono's pantheism and the drollery of Pagnol colored my dreams of Provence with hues taken from the palette of Van Gogh, Cézanne, or painters from Henry d'Arles by way of André Dunoyer de Segonzac and René Seyssaud to Pierre Ambrogiani. Not to mention the artists of the Riviera. Frédéric Mistral's "authentic" Provence, to which Daudet pays splendid tribute in letters in the guise of a pilgrimage to Maillane—the fundamentalists' Provence—is no doubt respectable, but a mite too regional for my taste. Too much patois, too much in the way of scholarly reconstitution. Among them I practically feel in a foreign country. Daudet goes right to the heart of things: olive groves, the symphony of the cicadas, the scent of lavender or rosemary, a curlew taking wing, heather lying like velvet. The Provence he conjures up beneath the sun has nothing esoteric about it; it is mine and belongs to whoever desires it. His *Letters* provide the key.

My own private Provence revolves around Fontvieille. Even if the windmill has been revamped for tourists, it remains unsullied. The emotion that seizes me accompanies me down the D17 road crossing the Paradou and Maussane on its way to Les Baux and Saint-Rémy, or to Eyguières, where I look for "the low house

Pages 176–77
"The concert of the cicadas made my head spin, the colors made my eyes pop—the green of the pastures, . . . the misty mauve of the mountainsides." D. T. Lavender in the Drôme, Provence.

Facing page
"Frédéric Mistral's 'authentic' Provence . . . is no doubt respectable, but a mite too regional for my taste." D. T. The statue of Mistral adorning the place du Forum in Arles in front of the legendary Nord-Pinus Hotel.

with gray shutters and a little garden behind" abutting the monastery. As a child I had tears in my eyes reading this love story: the heedless grandson, the arrival of his friend, the delight of the impoverished oldsters, the orphan girls, the lunch, the cherries in eau-de-vie with no sugar. You no longer look at your grandfather or grandmother with the same eyes once you've read *Les Vieux*. The same outpourings in the Camargue: every pond echoes with the description of the "hides" and the banks of the Vaccarès—the mysterious salt lake in which herds would occasionally drown.

Some scenes in *Letters from My Windmill* stray far from the sacred quadrant centered on the abbey at Montmajour. The two-horse boneshaker *patache* in the "Two Inns" starts from Beaucaire, while "the pope's mule" actually kicked out in revenge in Avignon. The stars in the "Zodiac" invented by the shepherd for the beautiful Stéphanette flicker under the sky over the Lubéron, while it is in a ghostly chapel at the summit of the Mont Ventoux that Dom Balaguère would say "Three Low Masses" for his redemption every Christmas Eve. No matter. I simply hang up the backdrops in the neighboring landscape of Fontvieille. Certain letters refer to Corsica—a lighthouse, a shipwreck, customs officers—and others to Algeria. This is Daudet flicking through the pages of his Mediterranean memories. The tales are well put together, no more; some I mix up, others I've forgotten. Meanwhile, around the mill, I expect at any moment to bump into Master Cornille carrying his sacks of plaster. I sympathize with his secret and curse industrial millers in a plausible allegory of a modernity that has left us bereft. Because, without really meaning to, the *Letters* revive a golden age of the countryside, a French myth if ever there was one. Before progress, before the rural exodus. I can just spot the prettily horned milk-white goat grazing on a slope of the Alpilles, and, as the sun goes down, the farmhouses dotted about the plain might once again belong to Monsieur Seguin. This goat whose tragic destiny offers a moral lesson to us all joins La Fontaine's animals in the schoolroom bestiary of France. The wolf that devours her inevitably evokes Charles Perrault's *Little Red Riding Hood*.

Almost inadvertently in his *Letters* Daudet goes beyond mere literary excellence and delights our imagination with a foundation myth. Or "re-foundation"; as you like. *Tartarin* and *Le Petit Chose* are masterpieces by a great writer of his time. Teachers now neglect them and soon, alas, nobody will read them anymore. But

Pages 180–81
"I can just spot the prettily horned milk-white goat grazing on a slope of the Alpilles." D. T.
"On the horizon, the slender ridge of the Alpilles.... And all this gorgeous Provence scenery lives only by dint of the light." Alphonse Daudet.

Facing page
"Arles, a marvelous little city, one of the most picturesque in all France." D. T.
This painting by Van Gogh, *Café Terrace on the Place du Forum* (1881), is one of his most famous.

"How was I not to
cast an envious eye on
this land of plenty, of
untamed nature... this
was enough exoticism
for me... a very French
patch of paradise." D. T.
Exoticism in the
quarries of Roussillon in
the Luberon separated
from the Alpilles by the
Rhône.

I fondly believe that *Letters from My Windmill* will not be forgotten any time soon. A deceptively childlike gem of our imaginary heritage, an epic for the lowly, it is also a heart-warming fairytale impregnated by spirituality, in which the farandole is danced to the sound of the tambourine. Writing these pages about the kingdom in which my childhood sought refuge, I reread these *Letters* for the *nth* time. Their magic remains intact, as does my desire to witness once more the landscapes they so transform.

In anticipation I shiver with delight seeing the bell towers emerge at a bend in the bypass:

Now come the ramparts of Arles. Squat ramparts with battlements, such as can be seen in old prints in which knights armed with lances appear at the top of a slope looking smaller than they do. We hurtle through this marvelous little city, one of the most picturesque in all France, with its carved, bulging balconies, jutting out like moucharabies into the middle of narrow lanes, with its ancient dark houses with low, pointed, Moresque doorways that take you back to the age of William the Short-Nose and the Saracens. At this hour no one is yet abroad. Only the Rhône quayside is bustling. The Camargue boat is getting up steam at the bottom of the steps, ready to set off. The tenant farmers are there in russet-red serge jackets and girls from La Roquette seeking work on a farm walk up on deck with us, chattering and laughing among themselves. Beneath long brown mantles folded up in the crisp morning air, the tall Arles headdresses makes their head look elegant and small, and beguilingly pert, as if they were standing taller so their laughter or waggery might be heard further. The bell sounds; we're underway. With the threefold speed of the Rhône, the propeller, and the mistral, the riverbanks fly by. On one side there is the Crau, an arid, stony plain. On the other, the verdant Camargue whose short grass and reed-strewn marshes extend out to sea.

I hesitate to take the steamboat today. Finally, I prefer to remain on the waterfront, watching the sun recompose the Arles skyline. Then I take the road to Fontvieille, the capital *ad vitam* of a Provence more real than the real one—mine, ours. A fabulous storyteller's ideal Provence.

It is a landscape where one feels happy because the range
of its colors is tuned in a tender and affectionate key,
because the lines are organized into a harmonious structure in
which it is pleasant to live. It is the most admirable of picturesques.

Jean Giono, *Provence*

───────────

"On the shoot for his film *Letters from My Windmill* after Alphonse Daudet,
Marcel Pagnol discovers his perfect accomplice: Jean Giono." Gaston Bonheur.

On the pleasant
shore of the French
Riviera... stands
a large, proud... hotel.
Deferential palms
cool its flushed facade,
and before it
stretches a short
dazzling beach.

F. Scott Fitzgerald,
Tender is the Night

Mealtimes

In this "global village," individual lifestyles are slowly being eroded. Even in France. It would seem, however, that one custom is bravely resisting standardization: mealtimes. Be it *en famille* or between friends, French eating rituals require a laid table and turned-off cell phones. At lunchtime, the demands of a job can reluctantly force the Frenchman to nibble a sandwich or a salad, alone or with colleagues, but, if he has time and the means, he will endeavor to lunch in a restaurant.

This, in general, is where contracts are signed, where professional ties are forged, where old friendships are rekindled. Business though is just an alibi: it was already done and dusted. The deal is closed only after coffee, the underlings being left to pore over the fine print. Nonetheless lunch served to seal the alliance, be it ever so provisional. When I used to ply the publishing trade, author signings required a freebie in a restaurant. The revival of a friendship that has petered out also calls for dining in town and, on saying goodbye, we always promise to "do it again soon." The same thing occurs toward the end of a meal with old pals from college, the barracks, the team, or the firm. The notion is practically written into the menu, and come dessert we are already plotting the next outing. Clubability—by nature at odds with French individualism—is only palatable over a groaning table. The same goes for summer shindigs. Finger-food and "preprandials" will often flow seamlessly into a full-blown banquet. People hunt round for chairs, a *saucisson* appears, then cheese, and by midnight you're peeling a fruit to finish off your glass of red.

In the evenings, ordinarily a French family will sit down at table for a dinner complete with first and second course, salad, cheese, and dessert. With or without wine, with or without television, but never in haste, and, all in all, conversation is known to occur. In this way people sustain a sense of being in a group that sociologists claim remains a telltale trait of French society. Be that as it may, this cult of mealtimes betrays the sacred nature of much that relates to food. Eating is far from anodyne; eating together verges, in consequence, on a religious act. Before they know how to read or write children learn they must not "get down" before dessert. Teenagers may squirm, especially if they feel the meal is dragging

Page 188
"An exotic boardwalk on which the palm trees never wither." D. T.

Facing page
"Mealtimes: a stretch of time during which family affection and understanding are sacred." D. T.
The country lunch immortalized by Robert Doisneau in 1948 was no hurried affair. The tablecloth is fully laid and the child is learning how to stay at table until dessert.

on forever, on Sunday for example, when kinship stretches to grandparents, uncles, and aunts. If hardly anyone attends Mass on Sundays, they'll still fetch the tablecloth from the closet, the bottles of aperitif out of the dresser, and Burgundy or Bordeaux from behind the woodpile. An open bottle for the humbler guests.

The same ceremonial goes with friends, dining out in a restaurant being one possible alternative. In France, be it at a wedding, a baptism, a first communion, a funeral, or a birthday, the moments of family life that really count are all marked at table in time-honored fashion. The feasts of our princes of the past have morphed into "Republican banquets." They go on and on, and, as course follows course, helped down by a good country red, "convictions" firm up: in the end though, we can't be that different as we partake of the same roast. Even with the young's get-togethers, though of course implying copious alcohol, there may be a meal in the offing, be it reduced to the specter of an oven-ready pizza.

The reason matters little, as long as we get to sit around a table. Not even the menu matters much, although the French are a congenitally foodie lot, good and heavy whenever possible. The essential thing is that stretch of time set aside for a feeling of conviviality that excludes haste and standing up, and that tolerates only gradual intoxication. A bulwark of privacy and family solidarity, it favors the blossoming of more understanding friendships. Seated at table in the remorseless spotlight of a nascent love affair, it may become clear, come the cheese, that the object of our desire is not quite the person we thought they were when they were cradling that aperitif. Without the initiatory ordeal of a candlelit dinner, one could have been sorely misled. At table in the evening parents tell each other about their day, abridged if necessary and observe their offspring out of the corner of their eye. In the office, at school, on a beach, or on the dance floor, one acts out a role. Unfolding a napkin, one opens the floodgates of one's soul. As long as the French eat seated at table, France will remain the preserve of a form of sociability that blends a delicate intimacy with outpourings of brotherly affection.

Right
"In France, be it at a wedding, a baptism, a first communion, a funeral, or a birthday, the moments of family life that really count are all marked at table in time-honored fashion." D. T.
Albert Auguste Fourié, *Wedding Meal at Yport*, Musée des Beaux Arts, Rouen.

The Riviera

I grant that the Riviera may today be nothing but a mirage. However, I fall for it as much as any one of the millions of ordinary Joes who still flood here every year. It might well be a sham, or worse, but I cannot bear to let a year pass without going on at least one excursion there. In winter, preferably, when the last mimosas, the first flowering cherries and bougainvilleas brighten up the dark green of the umbrella pines, the black cypresses, and the washed ocher of the houses. I return constantly and the same thrill of pleasure always washes over me, in the Var as much as in the Alpes-Maritimes. Each models its own Riviera out of the clay of our dreams.

Mine begins between the palm trees of Hyères and the Mayol stadium in Toulon, just behind the roadstead, in the quarter of Besagne. I have memories (of an affair) on the slopes of Faron and I have others (of friends) in Porquerolles.

Between Hyères and Bormes-les-Mimosas it's as ugly as hell. Then, brief glimpses of paradise until Rayol. Standing out between some trees belonging to a villa with which I have ties, the sea shimmers as if the hand of God had showered billions of diamonds upon it. One can watch the jibs dance and see the islands of Le Levant and Port-Cros. Saint-Tropez, Gassin, Ramatuelle, the Bay: all that remains beautiful, I tell myself with a sigh stuck in the car queuing for an hour to get on the peninsula. No less wonderful is the shoreline between Boulouris and Théoule-sur-Mer, with the red saw-toothed rocks of the Estérel against which the waves foam.

Cannes? More memories—a dinner in Suquet with Richard Anthony, doused in the nostalgia of a time when his hit songs drilled their way into my brain and I'd walk along the Croisette down to Palm Beach strutting my stuff like Alain Delon in the movie *Any Number Can Win*. Memories too of the Film Festival. More nuanced, as I always feel fake in a tux, an intruder among the "officials." Golfe-Juan: one thought for Napoleon, another for Cyril Connolly. The ramparts at Antibes, the steep streets, a riff by Sidney Bechet, the ghost of F. Scott Fitzgerald, the cathedral in a baroque resembling that of Sainte-Réparate in Nice or Saint-Pierre in Villefranche. After the pyramidal concrete horrors at Villeneuve-Loubet, the Baie des Anges.

In the end, I love Nice as much as Marseille. Just differently. It is no longer Provence, but it's not yet Italy. The views on the *moyenne corniche* road to Monaco have their purple passages. A detour via Villefranche never disappoints. And finally I like Monaco, a perfect mirage, more yellow than ocher. This is no longer France. And not Provence either. Even less the provinces, but not yet abroad. It is an operetta in which the heroines are all princesses. In Monaco everything is a stage-set, even the Louis II stadium on the rock from which the Grimaldis hang, suspended above the bay. To each their princess. The girls have those in the palace. I too have one, a friend, infinitely more beautiful than any cougar in a celebrity magazine in transit on one of the yachts that line the port. She is called Alexandra. Straw blond, as slender as a sapling, doe-like eyes, a smile that would send a Trappist to hell. When I enter a chic restaurant with her by my side, I feel like a non-resident-for-tax-purposes playboy. The impression doesn't last. I have neither the wallet, nor the taste, nor the physique for the role. But, for me, the heady glow of the Riviera, its languishing "Années Folles" side, is encapsulated in Alexandra.

This charm holds me in its thrall until Menton, which is a bit like a miniature model of Nice. I like to push on to Ventimiglia, a Naples-tinged Menton. It's raining in the Corrèze; it's winter. I close my eyes and I can picture a long scintillating garland of lights on the Croisette that starts at the peninsula at Giens and ends on the shore at Roquebrune, passing by the Baie des Anges.

The sea is blue, the sea is green. The sea is black, stars peck at the sky. Moving away from the littoral, the road climbs through sheer gorges, and I end up in a village perched on a hillside where pink houses squat behind the flowers. Back down again. The sea is still there. It's an unoriginal dream, but its sunlight warms the sleepless nights of many French and Englishmen, not to mention Dutch, Americans, and, nowadays, newly enriched Slavs.

Those dossing in the nearby campsites need not envy regulars at the Carlton, the Victoria, or the Hermitage: it is exactly the same dream. Or the same illusion, if you like. In the same cocktail-on-the-rocks, it mixes picture-postcards of Provence, an exotic board-walk down which the palm trees never wither, a free-and-easy sensuality, and a scintilla of relaxed elegance.

Tender is the night on the Riviera. Where all the men are transformed into Scott Fitzgeralds and all the women into Zeldas. Guaranteed enchantment.

Pages 194–95
"I grant that the Riviera may today be ... a mirage, but I cannot bear to let a year pass without going on at least one excursion here, in winter, preferably." D. T. Memories of Antibes with the snow-clad Alps in the background.

Facing page
"When I understood that every morning I would be seeing this light, I couldn't believe how happy I would be. I decided never to leave Nice." Matisse, 1917. Matisse painted *Flowers in Front of a Window* in 1922.

Pages 198–99
"What remains today of the Cap Ferrat where Gide came to flush out Malraux?" D. T. There remains these protected bays, like here at Saint-Jean-Cap-Ferrat.

I need the light, the air of Nice,
I need the Baie des Anges.

Friedrich Nietzsche

The Baie des Anges in Nice, bordered by the Promenade des Anglais.
Matisse, Nietzsche, and F. Scott Fitzgerald would throw open their windows
in the Hotel Beau Rivage over a then little-known bay.

So quietly flows the Seine
that one hardly notices
its presence. It is always there,
quiet and unobtrusive,
like a great artery running
through the human body.

Henry Miller, *Tropic of Cancer*

Saint-Denis Cathedral

The edifice itself is no great shakes. Like the Strasbourg Cathedral, it's missing a tower. Coming across Suger's great apse is therefore all the more staggering. Purity, simplicity, celestial luminosity: this is fledgling Gothic at its apogee. It's as if one is standing shoulder to shoulder with the throng of the pilgrims who come to pray here, before and since the construction of the basilica.

Longer ago still there was the tomb of Saint Denis, the exhortation of Sainte Geneviève, the age of the Merovingians. Some surviving sections of wall in the crypt date from around then. The crypt is a long-haul voyage across time: almost all of our kings, queens, and plenty of princes repose there. Some in Renaissance or Baroque mausoleums, others prone as *gisants*, under gravestones, or else embedded in the wall. Even that "Black Dog" du Guesclin has been permitted to enter the empyrean that overflows around the choir. The abiding sense, curiously, is not at all morbid: more like sauntering through a flowery garden. It makes no difference to know that the Revolution opened these tombs and tossed the bones into a common grave. Anyone who loves France has a lump in their throat, no matter what they think of these kings, who for the majority would have had me strung up if they had known my allergy to every form of power. This act of profanation opens the floodgates of the imagination, and one pictures the skull of Philip Augustus languishing *ad aeternam* beneath the limbs of Charles VII. The denizens are no longer good or vile: they just form part of this land's bountiful heart. I can smell it, and it sparks an outpouring of indistinct reminiscences and awakens images from schooldays, whether we read history books later on or not. All these kings tagged on to an adjective that makes them at once so mysterious and so familiar: the Bald, the Fat, the Good, the Wise, the Lion, the Mad, the Pious, the Fair, the Brave.

Emerging from the depths of the crypt, the contemporary world appears insubstantial, almost unreal. An avenue starts from the square down which walks a variegated crowd. This is Saint-Denis in the twenty-first century: Frenchmen from elsewhere, often from very far away indeed. Unknowingly, they keep alive the earliest period in our history, when people from many origins flowed in toward the basilica that had just been consecrated as a cathedral.

Sainte-Chapelle

This place—the upper chapel—is the sublime summit of French architectural heritage. Up a stone spiral staircase one enters a universe where the marvelous is par for the course, overwhelming the soul and transfixing the heart. In this forest of stained glass where red, blue, and gold scintillate in a celestial glow, one doesn't feel like praying, still less gawping. The religiosity it instills is both too ethereal and too pervasive: one is transmuted into a faithful believer from the age of Saint Louis. God is there, all around us, in us, and attested by the relics of the Passion of his Son, because this chapel is a reliquary: the king had to pay the patriarch of Constantinople hand over fist for the Crown of Thorns. The Seventh Crusade was in the offing and, if one had to lose one's life, one could wait here for the end of all things, inaugurated by Genesis and consummated on the Cross. The whole story is narrated in the stained glass; the epilogue, the apocalypse, is the subject of the rose window (late fifteenth century), where an ambivalent pale green modulates the ineffably shimmering blue, red, and gold. One can spend hours, days, years here gazing on the panels of the fifteen stained glass windows. And on the statues of the apostles with their cruciferous discs. Or on Christ blessing us from his trumeau. Or the Gothic flora on the capitals. One could devote one's whole life to the history of the Sainte-Chapelle, not to mention the nineteenth-century restorations. A tip of the hat to Viollet-le-Duc.

In this regard, the lower chapel in the form of a crypt, formerly for the parish of the Cité, represents a fine prelude to the dazzling event above, where only kings and noble guests would have had access. Art historians have their work cut out elucidating the mystery of this spirituality so spontaneously immanent and this light that changes in accordance with the time of day, the season, and the weather. This is the majestic France of the thirteenth century, that sets our patriotism in a sacramental halo: such is the upper chapel of the Sainte-Chapelle reliquary. The tourists queuing up with others trying to get into the appeals court next door on the graceless boulevard du Palais are only too right: up there, hushed silence reigns. Their meditation may not inevitably be religious, but in it lingers the vague, immediate consciousness of an authority of whose very existence they were, until then, unaware.

Page 202
"Paris. A silken mirage for lovers." D. T. Photograph by Willy Ronis in front of the Pont Royal, 1957.

Pages 204–5
"Almost all of our kings, queens, and plenty of princes of France repose in Saint-Denis." D. T. The *gisant* of Henry II.

Facing page
"A forest of stained glass where red, blue, and gold scintillate in a celestial glow." D. T.

Pages 208–9
The magical journey starts at the Pont de Sully in this photograph taken downstream from the Île de la Cité.

A Walk along the Seine

The journey begins at the Pont de Sully at the end of the Île Saint-Louis, with the splendid rounded tip of the Hôtel Lambert and the prow-shaped square and its monument to the sculptor Antoine-Louis Barye. One can admire the rhythms of the Quai de Bourbon, the Hôtel de Miramion, and the Hôtel de Nesmond on the Quai de la Tournelle. Then salute in passing the statue of Sainte Geneviève protecting a child and catch a glimpse between the islands of the lacework atop the Tour Saint-Jacques and the belfry of the church of Saint-Gervais. One can see too the dome of the Panthéon on a section of sky cut round by the waves of the rue de Bièvre whose tubby buildings seem to be concealing some secret from medieval times, only to go into ecstasies before the chancel of Notre-Dame and its splendid battery of flying buttresses. The rose window is so dazzling that we tend to forget the little square delectably shaded with plane-trees where the rue Maître-Albert flows into the Quai de Montebello. The Second Empire fountain on the place Saint-Michel is well worth a glance as is the turret on the Quai des Orfèvres. The pink brick buildings and white stringcourse of the place Dauphine are presently besieged by less attractive neighbors, marring its over-all elegance. Still, it remains a fine example of secular architecture from the beginning of the age of the musketeers, as testified by the two houses at the end of the Île de la Cité in front of the statue of Henry IV. Though the king ordained that the square should become the largest in all Europe, Ravaillac made sure this never came to pass. Instead, the nineteenth century inflicted upon Paris the Hôtel-Dieu, the Law Courts, and the Préfecture de Police.

Passing by the Hôtel de la Monnaie level with the Pont des Arts, the eye wavers between two gems: on the left, the Institut de France and on the right, the Louvre, whose frontage goes pink in the setting sun. The best time to drive along the riverside is when Paris is dressed for the night. In daytime, one lingers by the secondhand booksellers' stalls, one is drawn to the islands, or gets lost in the streets leading to the quays of the Left Bank with their architectural anthology of the fifteenth (Montebello), sixteenth (Grands-Augustins), and seventeenth (Conti, Voltaire) centuries. Some may not appreciate the converted station of Orsay: it has a bourgeois arrogance, but the museum lacks grace. With those on

Right
"The best time to drive
along the riverside is
when Paris is dressed for
the night." D. T.
The car passes beneath the
Pont Neuf just in front
of the tip of the Cité.

the Pont Alexandre III, the lampposts on the place de la Concorde conjure up a fairy realm that propels us back to the Belle Époque, as do the glass canopy and horses of the Grand Palais. Meanwhile, the parallel lines of the columns on the Palais Bourbon and the Madeleine take us back one more century. It is a relatively majestic neoclassicism, but without the genius that elevates the golden dome of the Invalides to the sublime. It effortlessly dominates the most beautiful Louis XIV monument (after Versailles) and one recalls that, behind the church of Saint-Louis with its forest of standards, lies the tomb of Napoleon. Him again.

There is hardly time to make out all the ghosts of French history quartered around Notre-Dame and the Louvre: the Middle Ages, the Renaissance, the classical period, and the modern age too, because every poet, every singer has versified on these august banks. Dazzled by the bluish glow of the *bateaux-mouches*, we progress through a kind of dream. The Alma, the Eiffel Tower, the Trocadéro, and that's the end of our little voyage. Further downstream the Seine has no more magic to reveal. It is worth returning to only in Troyes, Rouen, or Caudebec-en-Caux; the Pont Mirabeau no longer deserves the affection Apollinaire showered upon it in his poem, and the industrial era has more or less ruined what the impressionists beautified between the bridge at Sèvres and Mantes.

No other river can offer such a twenty-minute ride. If one focuses on the major sites, no less deserving is the apse of the oldest church in Paris, Saint-Julien-le-Pauvre, behind the square Viviani. One can even discern the arches of the chevet of the church of Saint-Séverin or the belfry of Saint-Germain l'Auxerrois. But there is scarcely time to take in the arches of the Pont Neuf, or linger on the Pont des Arts, from where the view over the Cité and the waterfront is enchanting. One feels inclined to do the trip again on foot, taking one's time to savor what is a complete kaleidoscope of the genius of French architecture.

Right
"The place Dauphine remains a fine example of secular architecture from the beginning of the age of the Musketeers, as testified by the two houses at the end of the Île de la Cité in front of the statue of Henry IV." D. T.
The square and the statue both appear in Renoir's *Pont Neuf, Paris,* 1872.

Page 214
Bernard Hinault won the Tour de France no less than five times. Photograph from 1985.

When the Tour de France passes,
France is on its doorstep.

Tristan Bernard

Bayeux Tapestry

Fascinating in its artless realism, the Bayeux Tapestry tells a story that is French, though not uniquely. A king in majesty (Edward the Confessor), Harold's expedition through Normandy, his meeting with William the (future) Conqueror, the Brittany countryside, Harold's oath, Edward's death, the appearance of Halley's Comet, boats built, then launched at sea, in full sail, the fortifications at Hastings, the battle, Harold killed. *Et fuga verterunt Angli* ("and the English fled") concludes the Latin text. The writer who scripted this masterpiece of secular Romanesque art has bequeathed a myth on a par with *The Song of Roland* and other tales of chivalry. The heirs to the founder of Normandy, Rollon, had to be French, and so it came to pass. Nonetheless, after Hastings, England became Norman, and, with a sprinkle of imagination doused in a dose of perfidy, one might retrospectively call England a colony. An independent one, naturally. Even prior to William's conquest and its settlement by his barons and clerks, a romanized Norman was already spoken at the court of England.

Taking advantage of an unverifiable oath by Harold, the precarious successor to old Edward (whose mother was Norman), the illustrious bastard triumphed at Hastings, was crowned in London, subjugating the country in the feudal manner. Thus a duke of Normandy, a vassal of the king of France, became a king of England. Likely commissioned by the bishop of Bayeux, Odon, William's half-brother, who was present at Hastings, perhaps the tapestry was woven in Kent. Or Winchester. Specialists have conjectured endlessly. This tapestry, over two hundred feet, long is probably unfinished since it omits the coronation of William. It does its utmost to preserve English pride: Harold is a true king, duly sporting a crown, and he falls honorably. However that may be, between Canterbury and the ancient kingdom of Wessex, I myself feel as if in a conquered land; it is a kind of Normandy over the Channel, as wooded as can be and peopled, not by Emma Bovarys, but by the delicious if less sensual heroines of Jane Austen.

Left
"This tapestry, over two hundred feet long, is probably unfinished." D. T.
The tapestry is listed by UNESCO World Heritage.

The TGV

I have been known to stand a few yards back from the ballast, somewhere among the pines of the Landes, and excitedly watch for its long, shark-like muzzle. Its sound is unlike that of other trains. The blue snake uncoils its rings, zooming past in a howl. The heart beats faster; it's amazing, but the mirage is already flying off and all one can see are two lights that quickly vanish, down on the rails. The beauty of the TGV is that of the Concorde. The lines of the fuselage are so pure they can only be compared to an orb by Brancusi, as if its increasingly delirious sophistication culminates in a return to elementary aesthetic prototypes. Recent regional trains now resemble a less tapering version.

If I take the TGV at Lyon, it takes me to Montchanin, Lausanne, Mouchard, Valence, or Aix-en-Provence. I am fond of these metal and glass country stations plonked down in the middle of nowhere. Waiting here has quite a different flavor from waiting in an ordinary station. Hardly has one emerged than one finds oneself in the midst of fields or woodland. I also like to get on at Montparnasse and hear, in a few hours, the accent of the Landes in the station buffet at Dax, or get off at Surgères, Ruffec (no buffet), or Auray. If God permits, I would like to visit all its stops. They are not so numerous and, though smoking is forbidden, I enjoying traveling by TGV; the once recognizable and novel landscapes it rushes past look different from ordinary fast trains.

Still, international prestige or no, one can lament the staggering mediocrity of the food you line up for in the refreshment "space." Since it always arrives on time, though, one is advised to exercise a little patience until one's destination, where one is sure to find a good eatery. There is only one major disadvantage: the "busy" exec dictating an email into his mobile and assaulting our eardrums, though some cars have signs requesting that passengers switch them off. Just this once, I'd like such a regulation to be respected. Another kind of bore: the loon with his ears plugged into his iPod listening to techno and lolling about like a bear at the zoo. But the TGV can't be held responsible for the vagaries of modern life. Its gentle roll should instead encourage one to sidle up to that girl daydreaming at the scenery as it hurtles past.

The TGV

Pages 218–19
The TGV and fashion:
two symbols of French
creativity. Ever stylish:
the TGV was five and
the Yves Saint Laurent
suit twenty when this
photo was taken for
Life magazine.

Right
The TGV flying through
"this spider's web whose
heart lies at Paris." D. T.

Tour de France

To tell the story of a stage on the Tour de France in the sports' daily *L'Équipe*, the journalist Antoine Blondin would borrow from the lyrical history of Michelet or from a medieval *chanson de geste*. In fact, with its sequence of initiatory ordeals, this July ritual that penetrates deep into the bowels of France is not unlike the quest for the Grail. A bouquet, a kiss, gold on the armet rewarded the bravest knight. Or the cleverest. Anyhow, they generally went hand in hand.

In former times, the roads were stony, sometimes snow-clad and a cyclist might meet a bear on a peak in the Pyrenees. Now the asphalt glitters. Everything is organized, marked out, policed, technicalized, but as before either of the World Wars, all the champion riders all dream of arriving in Paris in the yellow jersey, or at least of wearing it for a stage.

Even if he is no cycling fan, a Frenchman is sure to have watched the Tour pass by at least once, the day it ventured out into his region. Because the Tour has ended up traveling to the most remote country towns and covering the most deserted byways. People study the route in the local paper. Families or groups of buddies go along. Patiently, with joyful heart, they sit in ambush at the edge of the road. The ambience is that of a summer fete: chips, sausages, Bermuda shorts, ice cream for the kids, cans of beer for the guys. Gendarmes at every intersection. Here comes the caravan blaring music and spewing out balloons, showers of candy, and multicolored caps galore. Official cars and outriders whizz by in whistling cacophony. The wait turns feverish. They can't be far now. Rumor has it there's been a break. More race officials and whistles, and suddenly there appears just after the bend the stage leader, swinging side to side. Watches are consulted to calculate how far back the peloton is. Watching it swoop round the bend, I look for the yellow jersey. Everyone wants to see the yellow jersey. At worst, you kind of guess it's there. Nothing is over quicker than a peloton riding past. A few more race vehicles, three riders off the pace and the show's over. In a flash. You traipse home, a bit out of it, to watch the stage finish on TV. From a helicopter cameras film scenery and villages you thought you knew. Seen from the sky they gain in majesty. In embracing the modern age, the Tour de France has forfeited nothing of its heart.

Facing page
"All the champion riders dream of arriving in Paris in the yellow jersey, or at least of wearing it for a stage." D. T.
The riders photographed on rue de Rivoli by Martine Franck in 1980 can almost smell the finishing line on the Champs-Élysées.

Pages 224–25
"Nothing is over quicker than a peloton riding past. A few more race vehicles, three riders off the pace and the show's over. In a flash." D. T.
A drawing by the cartoonist Sempé from his album *Un peu de la France*.

This is not a palace,
but a city entire,
superb in its grandeur,
superb in its materials.

Charles Perrault

Versailles

Every time I return, I wonder what visitors from abroad must think. The "grandeur" the guides always talk about is typical of the reign of the Sun King: the pomp and circumstance of the Court, the mistresses, and the etiquette, the court comedies reported in Saint-Simon's *Memoirs*. I have no liking for old Louis XIV. If Versailles were simply the mirror of his majesty, I'd go somewhere else to enjoy a France no less proud, but less uptight. Because, with Saint-Simon's genial quill, the French language attains its apogee. In the masterpiece he unknowingly bequeathed us, what he relates is viewed through the prism of his vanity and is likely to have been experienced under every monarchy and during every republic.

Still, Versailles has always fascinated me. Not so much for its supposed opulence, although it bedazzled every other court and inaugurated a long cultural supremacy, imposing our language and our cast of mind. Yet in Versailles nothing really is imposing or even oversized. The magic of the place operates on a more familiar level, and, far from being intimidated or overwhelmed on walking up from the place d'Armes to the palace's Louis XIII frontage, I feel at home. Strolling around, and as soon as its other architectural face—that of Hardouin-Mansart—comes into view from the two Bassins, it is its charm that strikes us most. You just have to lose yourself (as a couple is best) in the maze of thickets by Le Nôtre, stroke the marble statues, or turn back to look down on Le Brun's Basin of Apollo to be gradually enveloped in its delightfully supernatural and gracefully fairylike ambience. You just have to saunter down to the Grand Canal and on to the Grand Trianon—but forget about the off-putting and misleading word, "grand." "Harmony" is a far more suitable term. This is the quintessence of French classicism and the zenith of the French baroque: restraint in sensuality, discretion in order and balance, rigor in luxuriance. It's as if the word "civilized," having miraculously discovered its perfect incarnation, decided it could advance no further. This is an emotion I feel especially strongly in the chapel, in the gilded salons, and down the whole length of the Hall of Mirrors. An apotheosis, certainly, but, in the final analysis, an understated, almost crepuscular one. It's a far cry from the sinister "grandeur" of the Escorial or the ramrod majesty

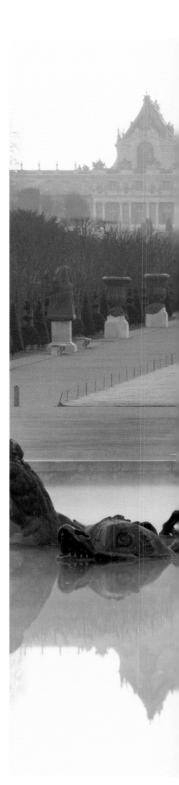

Page 226
"You just have to lose
yourself (as a couple
is best) in the maze of
thickets by Le Nôtre
and stroke the marble
statues." D. T.
Bacchante in the park
of the Château de
Versailles.

Pages 228–29
"As the walk unfolds,
we are enveloped by
charm... turning to
look back on the Basin
of Apollo." D. T.

Right
A view down the Hall
of Mirrors.
"An apotheosis,
certainly, but... an
understated, almost
crepuscular one." D. T.

of Schönbrunn, to make a comparison with two other acmes of the kind.

With Versailles, France addresses to the rest of the world the resplendent smile of a belle far too sure of her advantages to brag. France has been, at other times, nobler, more virtuous, more glorious, even, and notably younger. But never so gorgeous. This triumph of femininity swells our pride, as much as would a hundred feats of arms. Versailles is France in a state of grace, at the gleaming zenith of its genius, a temple of and to Frenchness.

I tend to be indulgent of Louis Philippe if only because the bright idea of converting the former apartments of the princes into a museum to our past glories—of every kind and under every regime—originated with him. This praiseworthy exercise in syncretism throws together statues of our writers, of our earliest kings, and our warriors, and portraits of our field marshals with family trees of the great families, David's *Coronation of Napoleon* and him again on the bridge at Arcole (by Gros), as well as crucial battles mythologized on canvas by Le Brun, Fragonard, Vernet, and Delacroix. Of course the "bourgeois king" did not forget himself, but this matters little: this whole ragbag of French history is as moving as the crypt of the kings in the Saint-Denis Cathedral. And it is only right that it should be hosted at Versailles, since it is here that France composed the opulent drama of an existence that has since kept the rest of the known world amazed.

Facing page
Around the pond in
the Queen's Hamlet:
a farm, a mill, a dairy,
fairy-tale thatched
cottages, and the
Marlborough Tower
from the summit of
which one can gaze down
on the entire hamlet.

Marie Antoinette was neither a great saint of royalty,
nor the great whore of the Revolution,
but an ordinary sort, an essentially average woman.

Stefan Zweig, *Marie Antoinette*

"It was in the year 1779 that I made the portrait of the queen
that shows her wearing a satin dress and holding a rose."
Élisabeth Vigée-Lebrun, *Souvenirs.*

Wine

"He who cannot drink knows nothing." Boileau

My oenological culture is patchy at best. I know the soils better than the grape varieties cultivated on them. The secrets of pinot noir, cabernet sauvignon, and merlot are quite safe with me. In blind tastings I cannot distinguish a Moulis from a Pauillac, I just about get that it's a Médoc. Is it as "supple" or as "well-structured" as they tell me? The acacia, vanilla, red fruits, and leather initiates detect go right over my head. Or, more precisely, I recognize them once I'm told they're there. I love wine and I appreciate an expert's view, as long it's not priggish or overly technical. Oenology interests me less than traveling among the vines and my taste buds tend to linger as much over the landscapes. If it is a Cahors, I snake along the *causse* near Montcuq or Prayssac, the village of Marshal Bessières (his heart lies in the church). If it's a Jurançon, I picture the bridge over the *gave*, or stream, from the boulevard of the Pyrenees, and my mind fills with memories of manly deeds in the stadium of Croix-du-Prince.

I cannot imagine drinking Tursan with a flame. It calls for buddies, rugby ones, if possible. I picture my belle sipping a flute of champagne, or at worse a glass of Saint-Julien or a Bonnezeaux.

A wine, a more or less languishing corner of undulating France, with its associated memories and the writers who have lauded it. I would be in a tight spot if asked to describe the wine of Saint-Michel-de-Montaigne. Does it deserve the appellation of Côtes-de-Castillon? Probably not, since the locality lies in the Dordogne. No matter. As it drink it, I see in my mind's eye the château on its headland, and the valley below, the park, Montaigne's famous tower, and I find parallels between the scenery, the nectar, and the open-hearted frankness of the *Essays*, their unbuttonedness, their panache.

If I'm served a Sauternes, it takes me into the world of François Mauriac, between Saint-Symphorien (*Le Mystère Frontenac*) and Malagar on its hill. A glass of Pouilly Fumé whisks me off to Tracy; a glug of Côte Roannaise commemorates a love (long dead) on the outskirts; the effervescence of a Vouvray brings me back to Balzac (*L'Illustre Gaudissart*), and the vivacity of a Chinon, to Rabelais. The little I do know, I owe to two friends, both

236

Wine

Facing page
"I know the soils better than the grape varieties cultivated on them. The secrets of pinot noir, cabernet sauvignon, and merlot are quite safe with me." D. T.

Pages 238–39
"Oenology interests me less than traveling among the vines and my taste buds tend to linger as much over the landscapes." D. T.
A Burgundy vineyard.

authors, and chalk and cheese: Kauffmann and Pirotte. Jean-Paul Kauffmann was released after three years of captivity in Lebanon. He looked round for a perch and landed at Pissos, in the Haute Lande, not far from Sore and Argelouse that both appear in novels by Mauriac. His cellar is a tabernacle, always kept under lock and key. He knows everything there is to know about wine. Thanks to him I learned the rudiments, glass in hand. I've met winegrowers, discovered the "2" B-road that slices through the peninsula of the Médoc from Margaux to the less exalted *cru bourgeois* vintages above Lesparre-Médoc. Inveterate dunce that I am, I retain only scraps of all this, and its jargon would soon put me off were it not for the poetry he adds, as well as a flabbergasting familiarity with history. Let's just say that my commerce with him has made me less hopeless, especially in respect of Bordeaux—the "wine of regret," as he calls it.

Jean-Claude Pirotte is less melancholic, but he lives in Arbois, and after a stopover in the Charentes and another in Cabardès, he has made it his job to promote Lotharingia: that is, the wines of Burgundy and the Jura. In his way an aesthete, a remarkable painter, as gifted in verse as in prose, like Kauffmann he possesses the gift of being able to set a wine—its *terroir*, vine variety, vintage—in its historical and literary context. He alerted me to several little-known poets whose stanzas he might recite between two digressions on the personality of a Pommard or a Montrachet. Kauffmann has it that these are more "immediate" wines, conjugated in the present indicative. "Catholic wines," as the eminent geographer Pitt calls them, in contrast with the Protestantism of Bordeaux. Catholic, since they historically burgeoned around monasteries and were long drunk in the Vatican. But French too: Paris was their natural outlet and they were poured in the Louvre, in the Tuileries, and at Versailles.

Bordeaux on the other hand is more cosmopolitan: since forever it has been dispatched to England and Scandinavia. If I ventured an opinion of a not very enlightened amateur, I would add that Burgundies tend to be merrier and more casual. Hence my sympathy (and taste) for little vintages of white Côte de Macon and red Côte de Nuits; their intoxication feels more fraternal. I am not a fountain of knowledge like Kauffmann or Pirotte, I never will be. Still, I think of my sojourns at Pissos and Arbois as celebrations of a complex magic that blends developing expertise and a rootedness in history and geography with an intelligent use of the senses.

Volcanoes

I can see volcanoes right out of my window. Their peaks turn blue in the setting sun. I sometimes take it into my head to scale an extinct cone, and up there, high above than the pastures dotted about with russet-red cows and black bilberries, on the almost lunar roof of the Auvergne, thoughts wander to origins and ultimate destiny. It seems the rugged Auvergne is conducive to spirituality: spanning three centuries of Cartesianism, Pascal and Teilhard de Chardin hail the union between science and mysticism. Two denizens as unyielding as the black lava that bestows a particular majesty on the cathedral in Clermont and the town of Riom. Such places, more than elsewhere, make one feel disinclined to futility.

Pascal, Teilhard: two pillars of my humble metaphysics. Pascal infused into my mind at the age when my buddies were groping around reading Sartre. *Les Pensées* are a monument—unfinished, neglected—of French thought. One can skirt round Pascal: but one cannot rattle him nor unseat him. On the question of grace, I side with the Jesuits rather than his pals, the Jansenists. But Pascal was right in being wrong: Jansenist pride, his dissident spirit, his moral rectitude gave rise to a glorious moment of French spirituality.

On the other hand, it was wrong for the Jesuits, with a nod from the Vatican, to persecute the greatest of them all: Teilhard. In penance for its blindness I hope the Church canonizes him one day: he was the only one to overlay the befuddled Hegelianism that replaces guidance in our age with a veneer of hope. This gloriously handsome aristocrat would always have been a solitary hero. He found God in the depths of his heart and in tramping the scree in far-flung Tibet. He loved a lady with the purest, but most eminently human, love. He could have broken the vow that condemned him to prevaricate in his effort to forge a theology that would make neither scholars nor philosophers laugh. He wavered, but never broke. Through faithfulness and humility. The novel of his life sends me into transports of admiration; the epilogue in New York fills me with sadness. After succumbing to Pascal's pessimism, Teilhard can fill me with optimism. These two undying Auvergne volcanoes present two sides of the same coin. Two French geniuses. Two Arverns as rebellious as Vercingetorix. Two watchtowers in the dark night of our uncertainty.

Facing page
"On the Puy de Sancy, from which one takes in the hills and dales of a landscape of infinite horizons. The almost lunar roof of the Auvergne." D. T.

Pages 244–45
"At the foot of the volcanoes, Salers, with its *lauze* roofing-tiles and its turrets of black basalt, recalls the mysteries of the Middle Ages." D. T.

It is easier to change
religion than it is
to change cafés.

Georges Courteline

The *Zinc*

Push open the door and lean an elbow on the bar. Order a coffee, a *crème* or *noisette*. Grab a croissant from the basket while standing next to a deliveryman sipping a small glass of chilled white. Light a cigarette, puff on it, and blithely observe the passersby from behind the pane of glass. Stamp out the cigarette on the floor. To the left, in the rear, the toilets, sometimes of the "squat" variety. In larger brasseries, they are in the basement, next to the payphone. The *zinc*—the counter or bar—is no longer made of zinc. On occasion it might be copper, but it remains a harbor for walker and worker alike.

Some bars also sell tobacco, papers, and mags, possibly betting slips. Above all in the provinces. The "Gottlieb" pinball of my youth has been replaced by sophisticated electronic devices with consoles and player rankings. All too often, a TV screen shows idiotic pop videos on a loop; or soccer, which is better, but all the same it adulterates the blissful vacuity of the mind. Outside, the city goes about its business. A pensioner by the cash desk is choosing the runners and riders. The owner flicks through the newspaper and lets fly a passably populist observation such as: "They're all on the take." The waiter wipes down the counter with a cloth; the proprietress is hard at work before the percolator. Outside, time passes quickly; at the *zinc*, it edges past. After the morning glass of white come balloons of red or halves of beer for the plasterers and painters on the nearby building site. Smokes. A bawdy joke shakes the proprietress out of her torpor. The proprietor has that twinkle in his eye. Customers thin out. The counter becomes the refuge for a hobo and a lush, eyes dulled by the abuse of loneliness. Suddenly, it's aperitif time. Not the real one—its midday ersatz when there's never "one for the road." Two hours spent marking time, then, in bowl the high-school kids, seldom at the counter, though. They sit, with a Diet Coke for the girls and a beer for the boys. Then, finally, the real after-work snifter, regulars straight from their toil. "A Ricard." "Same again?"

A French bar offers punters a dose of warmth, silent or vocal, protected from the daily grind. The French like hanging out in bistros. They are unlike a Viennese café, English pub, German tavern, or even an Italian coffee bar. Leaning on the *zinc*, a Frenchman always feels more than just a customer.

Page 246
"The *zinc*—the counter or bar—is no longer made of zinc. On occasion it might be copper, but it remains a harbor for walker and worker alike." D. T.

Facing page
"At the bar, if one appropriates, incorporates a fraction of the bistro, one remains in complicity with the outside." D. T. Author Marcel Aymé preparing a *citron pressé* at the bar.

Photographic Credits

The publisher has endeavored to contact copyright holders and obtain their permission
for the use of copyright material. In the event of any error or omission, the publisher
would be grateful if notified, and will rectify any inadvertent omissions in future printings.

By the same author

À la santé des conquérants. Paris: Robert Laffont, 1984.

L'Ange du désordre: Marie de Rohan, duchesse de Chevreuse. Paris: Robert Laffont, 1985.

Le Bar des palmists. Paris: Arléa, 1989.

Le Bonheur à Souillac. Paris: La Table Ronde, 2001.

Boulevard des Maréchaux. Paris: Le Dilettante, 2000.

Cholley, le grand guerrier. Toulouse: Privat, 2011.

Chirac-Hollande, une histoire Corrézienne. Paris, Plon, 2014.

Considérations inactuelles. Paris: Plon, 2012.

La Corrèze et le Zambèze. Paris: Robert Laffont, 1990.

Dernier verre au Danton. Paris: Robert Laffont, 1996.

Dictionnaire amoureux de la France. Paris: Plon, 2011.

Le Dieu de nos pères. Paris: Bayard, 2004.

Don Juan. Paris: Robert Laffont, 1998.

Du bonheur d'être réac. Sainte-Marguerite sur Mer: Equateurs, 2014.

Elvis, balade sudiste. Paris: La Table Ronde, 1996.

En désespoir de causes. Paris: Gallimard, 2002.

L'Été anglais. Paris: Robert Laffont, 1983.

L'Hôtel de Kaolock. Paris: Robert Laffont, 1991.

Incertains désirs. Paris: Gallimard, 2003.

L'Irlandaise de Dakar. Paris: Robert Laffont, 1986.

Je me souviens de Paris. Paris: Flammarion, 1998.

Je nous revois. Paris: Gallimard, 2006.

Le Jeu de la chandelle. Paris: Robert Laffont, 1994.

Juste un baiser. Paris: Guéna, 2012.

Un léger malentendu. Paris: Robert Laffont, 1988.

Maisons de famille. Paris: Robert Laffont, 1987.

Les Masques de l'éphémère. Paris: La Table Ronde, 1999.

Le Mystère Simenon. Paris: La Table Ronde, 2003.

Remembering Paris. Paris: Flammarion, 1998.

Le Retour de d'Artagnan. Paris: La Table Ronde, 1992.

Le Rêveur d'Amériques. Paris: Robert Laffont, 1980.

Rue Corneille. Paris: La Table Ronde, 2009.

Rugby blues. Paris: La Table Ronde, 1993.

Spleen à Daumesnil, followed by *Le tour des îles.* Paris: Le Dilettante, 1985.

Spleen en Corrèze. Paris: La Table Ronde, 1997.

Le Venin de la mélancolie. Paris: La Table Ronde, 2004.

Vichy. Seyssel: Champ Vallon, 1986.

Pages 252–53
"This is the heart of the Landes, the pines close off the horizon and suddenly Solférino emerges, scattered parts of the model farm designed by Napoleon III, a mirage of harmony between the trees." D. T.

Facing page
"*Remembering Paris* is a book I wrote in 1998, illustrated with paintings by the late lamented André Renoux, who loved Paris." D. T.
Here, the arcades on the rue Vaugirard, opposite the Luxembourg Gardens.

This book is an abridged and illustrated edition of the original work
published in French by Éditions Plon in 2011.

Editorial Director: Ghislaine Bavoillot
Original Layout Design: Isabelle Ducat
Translated from the French by David Radzinowicz
Editorial Coordination and Copyediting: Marc Feustel
Typesetting: Gravemaker+Scott
Proofreading: Bronwyn Mahoney
Color Separation: IGS, France
Printed in Spain by Grafos

Simultaneously published in French as *Dictionnaire amoureux de la France, version illustrée*
© Plon & Flammarion, S.A., Paris, 2014

English-language edition
© Plon & Flammarion, S.A., Paris, 2014

editions.flammarion.com

14 15 16   3 2 1

ISBN: 978-2-08-020209-3

Dépôt légal: 10/2014